# Classic Knits
## for
# Boy Dolls

Marjory Fainges

Kangaroo Press

Dedicated to all the knitters who just love to knit,
and in particular to make doll's clothes for their own
and other people's dolls.

*Acknowledgments*
Thanks to Dorothy and Jane Coleman of the United States
for first sowing the seeds for a book such as this; Jacki
Brooks (*Australian Doll Digest*) and Helen Whelan, both
of New South Wales, Lynn Riddell-Robertson and Barbara
(Hobby House Books), both of Victoria, for their encour-
agement; all the hoarders and lovers of dolls and knitting,
particularly those who are meticulous about dressing dolls
in the right clothing for their era; Shirleyanne McKay of
New South Wales for her help in soliciting some wonderful
old patterns from friends; Ross Schmidt and Sue Leighton-
White (Sanshi) of Western Australia for their help with old
and rare patterns; two wonderful people, Peggy Beer and
Joan Arkell of Queensland, who helped with the proving
of the patterns as a double check after I had knitted all the
garments and written up the instructions; Gwenda Spencer
who kindly loaned some of her collection of dolls to add
variety to the photographs. A special thanks to my husband
Jim who made some of the props and also cooked some of
the meals while I worked on the final type-up.

*First published in 1995 by Kangaroo Press Pty Ltd*
*3 Whitehall Road Kenthurst NSW 2156 Australia*
*PO Box 6125 Dural Delivery Centre NSW 2158*
*Typeset by Midland Typesetters Pty Ltd*
*Printed in Hong Kong by South China Printing Co. (1988) Ltd*

ISBN 0 86417 717 9

# Contents

# *Foreword*

With so many books on the market catering for the home knitter and crocheter of dolls' garments, how wonderful that at last here is one devoted entirely to boy dolls!

The author, Marjory Fainges, an acknowledged world authority on the history of dolls and toys, has thoroughly researched the history of all of the garments presented here. Each of the fifteen patterns is authentic in design and most suitable for antique boy dolls—and looks adorable on teddies too! Modern boy dolls can be given that classic look with one of the outfits featured in this book.

Marjory Fainges, an associate editor of the *Australian Doll Digest*, has spent many years researching the history of dolls, especially the history of the Australian doll makers. Titles to Marjory's credit to date are *Australian Doll Makers, A History* (1986), *Australian Costume, 1788–1988, for Teen Dolls* (1987), *Antique Dolls of China and Bisque* (1991), *Encyclopedia of Australian Dolls* (1993) and *Encyclopedia of Regional Dolls* (1994).

For too long the girl dolls have been catered for and pandered to—now it is time for the boys to shine in their new costumes!

The simple instructions of these patterns are suitable for the advanced or beginner knitter and will ensure that your boy doll will be the envy of all!

Jacki Brooks
Editor in Chief, *Australian Doll Digest*

# Introduction

The growth in doll collecting, coupled with the growing interest in handcrafts of all kinds, has led to many collectors around the world wanting to dress their antique, collectible and more modern dolls in the type of clothing they were dressed in when they were made, and a worldwide search has begun for suitable patterns.

In years gone by many dolls were sold without clothing, and then were lovingly dressed by parents and grandparents, very often in knitted outfits. Many older doll collectors and knitters will have fond memories of their childhood, when they had only one doll, or maybe two if they were lucky (during the Depression and the war years). Those precious dolls would sometimes receive a full wardrobe of clothes (carefully made from the plethora of knitting patterns then available) as part of their owner's Christmas or birthday present. Having myself been interested in knitting for fifty years or so, and taught by two excellent teachers, my mother and grandmother, to not only read knitting and crochet patterns, but to experiment with them, and also being a person who collects and files away information of all kinds, I have amassed quite an assortment of old knitting patterns for dolls over the years. Through the generosity of people such as Shirleyanne McKay, Ross Schmidt and Sue Leighton-Smith, who have so kindly added to my growing files over the last few years, I am able to present some of this vast amount of accumulated information for all to enjoy. One of the more interesting aspects of my collection is the number of patterns that were designed and printed in Australia which are different to those collected from overseas.

## Why clothes for boy dolls?

Talking to a large cross-section of doll collectors both in Australia and overseas, and asking what type of clothes they were looking for and couldn't find, it was remarkable the number who asked, 'Do you have any clothing patterns suitable for boy dolls?' This demand gave rise to this book, which gives both doll collectors and the average interested knitter a series of outfits suitable for boy dolls dating from the 1900s to the 1960s, varying in size from 17 cm (6½") to 48 cm (19") overall. My method of altering size means that each pattern can cover a much wider range of sizes than is apparent at first glance.

## Proving old knitting patterns

As both the denier size or thickness of the wool ply, and the method of writing knitting pattern instructions, have changed greatly over the years, and as many of the old patterns had mistakes in them (such as the suitability of the pattern to the number of stitches required, or lines of pattern omitted), I have had to prove every one of the patterns in this book before passing them on to two friends, Peggy Beer and Joan Arkell, who kindly and willingly knitted and recorded either smaller or larger versions of each pattern.

## Altering the size of a pattern

Several of the outfits included here will fit 36 cm (14") dolls; a number of others will fit 46 cm (18") dolls. Using a combination of garments from different patterns will give an even greater variety. Other outfits are portrayed on dolls that may be of a different size, shape and period, and it is here that my instructions differ from the norm; instead of giving the number of stitches required for a bigger size, I have for simplicity used the difference that a variation in ply and size of needles can give to produce the required sizes for different dolls. Thus with no extra effort, following the examples given in these instructions, clothing for larger or smaller dolls can be made from any of the patterns given, just by adjusting the size of the needles and the wool or yarn used.

If you like a pattern which is too small for your large doll, you can change to 5-ply wool and bigger needles, such as 4 or 4.5 mm (No. 8 or No. 7) (US size 6 or 7), or even larger sized wool and needles. The garment will be much bigger than the original, without having to change the number of stitches and rows. On the other hand, knitting a pattern with 1 mm (No. 16) or finer needles and very fine wool or yarn, such as 1-ply, will give you much smaller finished garments.

This is why the instructions for the patterns are all given in rows, not measured in centimetres or inches. As long as you change the wool or yarn size in proportion with the needle size, the garments will remain in true proportion.

# Tension

As some knitters work more loosely (or more tightly) than others, I suggest that you work a trial piece of knitting, 10 sts by 10 rows, to see if you are using the tension recommended in the pattern. If your sample has more stitches or rows than in the pattern, use needles a size smaller; use needles a size larger if your sample has less stitches or rows. If you are an uneven knitter here is a little hint—knit your purl rows using a size larger needle than in your knit rows—it works.

# Needle sizes

All instructions are given in both metric and imperial measurements, with both Australian/English and US sizes of knitting needles or crochet hooks specified.

# Wool or other yarns?

I have used woollen yarn throughout the book, mainly because wool was the medium used in the original patterns. For many of the patterns I have used Patons 3-ply Baby Wool or 4-ply Patonyle, both because Coats Patons have kindly given me permission to use patterns for boy dolls from knitting books they published from the late 1940s through to the 1970s, and also because these wools are readily available.

For other patterns I used Bendigo 2-ply and 3-ply fingering wool, which are both available in quite a wide range of both subdued and vibrant colours. This wool is easily available by mail order direct from the Bendigo Woollen Mills in Bendigo, Victoria (they take most credit cards also), or from their overseas distributors (see page 61 for addresses). In the patterns that I have designed myself, I have used both makes of wool to show the versatility of what can be achieved.

Other wools or yarns, such as those based on nylon, can readily be used. My only suggestion is that you start by making the smallest garment in an outfit to check what difference in size, if any, the different yarn may produce.

# Knitting terminology

A very important side to knitting is knowing what all the different terms and abbreviations mean. These are covered fully on page 10. For American knitters I have included a small but concise translation of the differences in crochet terminology, because simple crochet is used for the finish of some garments.

# Garment size and your doll

The sizes of the actual garments are given in both metric and imperial measurements, so all you have to do is measure your doll in the appropriate places, regardless of its age, to see whether the garment you have chosen will fit, using the materials given. You may have to change the size of wool and needles, always remembering that *knitted clothes stretch*, and thus can fit a doll bigger than the actual measurements given.

# Choosing appropriate patterns

Where possible in the photographs I have used dolls of an age in keeping with the age of the original patterns, but I have also shown more modern dolls wearing the same outfits. As all these patterns are classic patterns for boy dolls, they can really be used on dolls of any age.

# Finishing the garment

To press or not? Pressing is a very important part of giving the finished garment a professional look. If you have used pure woollen yarn, gently press (not iron) each piece of the garment before sewing up, either with a steam iron at a low steam temperature, or using a medium heat iron on a slightly damp cloth placed over the garment piece.

*Do not* heat-press any garment made from nylon or bri-nylon yarn.

I hope you get as much enjoyment from knitting these garments as I have, both from researching and making them. Some of your boy dolls can now be attired in a new suit of clothing, instead of wearing a girl's outfit or sitting naked at the back of the cupboard, waiting for the day a pattern for a suitable outfit can be found. Happy knitting.

# How to Knit

(or Knitting for Beginners, courtesy of Patons Woolcraft)

**Casting-on—making the first loop**

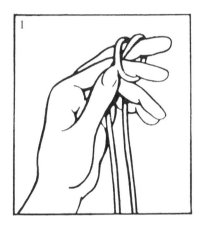 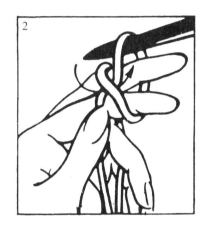 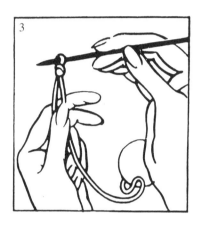

1. Wrap the yarn around the first and second fingers of the left hand.
2. Place point of needle under the front loop and draw back loop through.
3. Withdraw fingers from loop and draw loop up onto needle

**Casting-on using thumb and one needle**

4. Using the thumb and one needle, and working with a length of yarn sufficient for the required number of sts in your left hand, pass the yarn around the left thumb.
5. Place point of needle beneath the loop on the thumb, drawing loop up slightly.

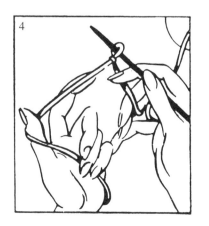 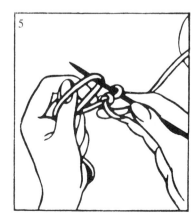

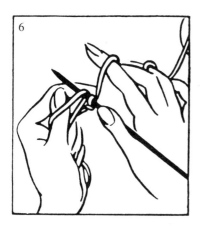
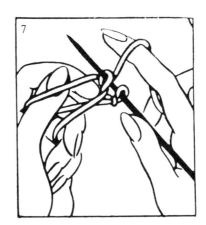
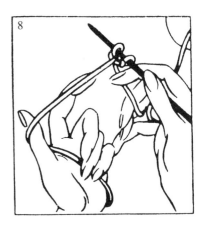

6. Hold yarn from ball in right hand ready to pass around the point of the needle.
7. Wrap yarn from ball around the point of the needle and draw through loop on thumb.
8. Draw up stitch on needle, pull both ends of yarn firmly, and repeat from step 1 until sufficient stitches have been cast on.

*Points to watch:*
- An even cast-on is essential to good knitting.
- Avoid casting-on too tightly, otherwise edge will not hang properly.
- This form of casting-on does not necessitate knitting into the back of the cast-on stitches.
- This method can be used for all general purposes.

**Casting-on—using two needles**

Make a loop (following diagrams 1 to 3), then place the point of the right-hand needle through the loop on the left-hand needle. Holding the yarn in the right hand, wrap the yarn around the point of the right-hand needle and draw the yarn through the loop on the left-hand needle, forming a second loop. Place this loop onto the left-hand needle (diagram 9). Now place the point of the right-hand needle *between the two loops on the left-hand needle.* Wrap the

yarn around the end of the right-hand needle (diagram 10) and draw a loop between the two loops on the left-hand needle. Place this loop onto the left-hand needle. Put the point of the right-hand needle between the first and second loops on the left-hand needle (counting from the point). Repeat until the required number of stitches have been cast on.

*Points to watch*
Keep the stitches on the left-hand needle near to the point. The yarn should come *over* the first finger of the right hand, *under* the second, *over* the third and *under* the fourth. The yarn should pass easily through the fingers, but should be held firmly to maintain an even tension.

**Knitting a stitch**

Hold the needle containing the cast-on stitches in the left hand. Insert the right needle from left to right through the first loop, pass the yarn around the point of the right-hand needle, draw a new loop through and, retaining this loop on the right-hand needle, slip the first loop off the left-hand needle (diagram 11).

In plain knitting the wool or yarn is always held at the back of the work. More than one row of knitting stitch creates the pattern known as garter stitch (diagram 12).

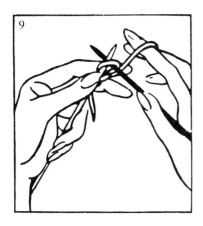
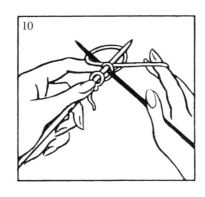
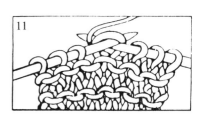

## Purling a stitch

Holding the yarn or wool to the front of the work (this is essential when purling), insert the right-hand needle from right to left through the first loop on the left-hand needle, pass the yarn around the point of the right-hand needle, draw the loop so formed through stitch onto right-hand needle and drop stitch off left-hand needle. Repeat this action across row (diagram 13).

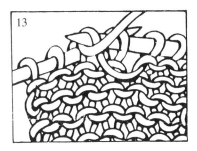

## Stocking stitch

By knitting one row and purling the next row a plain smooth pattern is created—this is known as stocking stitch or st st. The side facing you when you work the knit row is usually the right side of the work. Thus the purl side will be the wrong side (unless otherwise stated in the pattern). See diagram 14.

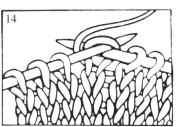

## Casting off

Knit the first two stitches, *insert the point of the left-hand needle from left to right through the first of these two stitches, slip this stitch over the second one, that is, take it off the right-hand needle, thus leaving one stitch on the right-hand needle (diagram 15).

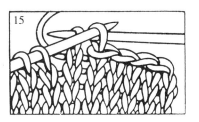

Knit the next stitch and repeat from * until only one loop remains. Break off the yarn and draw the end through the loop of the last stitch. Thread yarn through a yarn needle and darn it neatly into the work.

*Important* Unless otherwise stated, the edge formed by the cast-off stitches should be as elastic as the remainder of the garment.

When casting off at the beginning of a row (e.g. at the armholes) remember that if 6 sts are cast off, for example, 7 will be needed and used in order to cast off the 6th. This 7th st, therefore, has not been disposed of and must be included in the number of stitches left on the row, and must be counted as the 1st of such stitches.

## Tension

The simplest method of measuring tension is to cast on 20 sts using the size of needle and the yarn specified in the pattern (over smooth fabric), knit a square and press lightly. Check the tension by placing a measuring tape along the stitches, marking 2.5 cm (1") with pins and counting the exact number of stitches within the measured length.

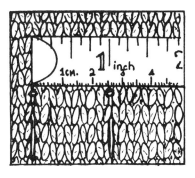

# Useful Information

## Wool thicknesses

| Australian | American |
|---|---|
| 2-ply | 2-ply fingering |
| 3-ply | 3-ply fingering |
| 4-ply | 4-ply fingering |
| 5-ply | |

## Knitting needle sizes

| Metric (mm) | Imperial | American |
|---|---|---|
| 2.0 | 14 | 0 |
| 2.5 | 13–12 | 1 |
| 3.0 | 11 | 2–3 |
| 3.5 | 10 | 4 |
| 3.75 | 9 | 5 |
| 4.0 | 8 | 6 |
| 4.5 | 7 | 7 |
| 5.0 | 6 | 8 |
| 5.5 | 5 | 9 |
| 6.0 | 4 | 10 |
| 6.5 | 3 | — |
| 7.0 | 2 | 10½ |
| 7.5 | 1 | — |

## Crochet hooks

| Metric (mm) | Imperial | American |
|---|---|---|
| 2.0 | 14 | B/1 |
| 2.5 | 12 | C/2 |
| 3.0 | 10 | D/3 |
| 3.5 | 9 | E/4 |
| 4.0 | 8 | F/5 |
| 4.5 | 7 | G/6 |
| 5.0 | 6 | 4/8 |
| 5.5 | 5 | I/9 |
| 6.0 | 4 | J/10 |
| 7.0 | 2 | — |

## Abbreviations and terminology

| | |
|---|---|
| * * | repeat instructions between * * |
| **** | refer back to previous section of pattern |
| alt | alternate |
| beg | beginning |
| C | contrast, or lesser colour used in two-colour knitting |
| dec | decrease—work 2 sts tog to form 1 st |
| g | gram/s |
| garter st | work every row in knit stitch |
| inc | work twice into st to make 2 sts |
| in | inch(es) |
| k | knit |
| m1 | make a stitch by placing wool over needle before the next st |
| MC | main colour used in two-colour knitting |
| mm | millimetre |
| ms | moss stitch—work k1, p1, alternately in following rows to give a broken rib effect; usually worked on an uneven no. of stitches. |
| no. | number |
| oz | ounce/s |
| p | purl |
| psso | pass the slipped stitch over |
| rep | repeat |
| rib | usually either k1, p1, or k2, p2, normally worked on an even no. of stitches, repeated to end of row |
| rib | in the case of garter st, the number of raised rows showing on one side of knitting |
| sl or sl st | slip the stitch onto needle |
| st/s | stitch/es |
| st st | stocking st—working one row in knit st and following row in purl st |
| tog | working 2 sts together to form 1 st |
| turn | reverse the way of knitting by working back on the needle just worked |
| wl fwd | bringing wool to front of work, before working next st, thus making a st; used in patterns and for small buttonholes |

10

# Handy hints

1. Knit through back of stitch on all cast-on stitches, using the two-needle method, to give a firm edge, particularly when this method has been used for making a buttonhole.
2. When picking up a stitch, pick up and knit before transferring it onto other needle.

# Equivalent crochet terms

| Australian/European | American |
|---|---|
| ch (chain) | = ch (chain) |
| sl st (single crochet) | = sl st (slip st) |
| dc (double crochet) | = sc (single crochet) |
| tr (treble) | = dc (double crochet) |

# Old knitting books

Some Australian readers may have old Patons knitting books which include patterns for dolls' clothes. Coats Patons have supplied the years of publication but advise that these books are now *out of print*, and cannot be obtained from the company or its outlets.

| Book No. C.3 | Published before 1950, reprinted 1950 |
|---|---|
| C.4 | Reprinted 1954 |
| C.5 | Published 1953, reprinted 1955 |
| C.8 | Published 1955, reprinted 1957 |
| C.12 | Published 1958 |
| C.13 | Published 1959 |
| C.14 | Published 1960 |
| C.18 | Published 1963 |
| C.23 | Published 1970 |
| C.26 | Published 1971 |
| C.28 | Published 1972 |
| C.38 | Published 1979 |

# Care of woollen garments

It takes only a little effort to give knitted garments the care they deserve, especially those made of natural fibres such as pure wool. Make the care regular and you will be rewarded with fresh, new looking clothes for a lifetime.

*2-ply, 3-ply and 4-ply wool fingering, and other pure woollen yarns*
Warm hand wash only in approved detergent.
Do not rub.
Do not bleach.
Warm rinse well—rinsing is essential.
Normal spin.
Do not tumble dry.
Dry flat and protect from direct sunlight.
Warm iron.
If drycleaning is required, P.50°C is the highest temperature needed.

*Baby wool*
Read the instructions as many baby wools are now machine washable.
Warm machine wash, short gentle cycle in approved detergent.
Do not rub.
Do not bleach.
Warm rinse well—rinsing is essential
Normal spin.
Do not tumble dry.
Dry flat—protect from direct sunlight
Warm iron
(Instructions courtesy Bendigo Woollen Mills.)

# *Anthony* *illustrated on page 17*

Easy to make, this two-piece outfit of jumper and pants, which will fit a 40–46 cm (16"–18") doll, was adapted from the 1932 edition of *Dress Your Dolly in Knitting and Crochet* by Ella Allen. Although ideally suited to a celluloid, composition or bisque (china) headed baby doll or toddler, this outfit is equally at home on a much more modern doll.

## LARGER DOLL

### Materials
50 g (2 oz) Bendigo 3-ply fingering wool
Smaller ball contrast colour
Pair 3.75 mm (9) (US 5) needles
Pair 3 mm (11) (US 3) needles
3.5 mm (9 or 10) (US E) crochet hook
Snap fastener (press-stud)
Length of elastic for pants

### Measurements
| | |
|---|---|
| *Jumper* Length from top of shoulder | 16 cm (6½") |
| Width around at underarm | 33 cm (13") |
| Length of sleeve seam | 7.5 cm (3") |
| *Pants* Length at centre front | 11 cm (4¼") |
| Length of inside leg | 4.5 cm (1¾") |

### Tension
14 sts in width, 14 rows in depth = 2.5 cm (1")

## SMALLER DOLL

### Materials
25 g (1 oz) 3-ply baby wool
Small ball contrast colour
Pair 3 mm (11) (US 3) needles
Pair 2.25 mm (13) (US1) needles
3 mm (11) (US D) crochet hook
Snap fastener (press-stud)
Length of elastic for pants

### Measurements
| | |
|---|---|
| *Jumper* Length from top of shoulder | 13 cm (5¼") |
| Width around at underarm | 25 cm (9½") |
| Length of sleeve seam | 5 cm (2") |
| *Pants* Length at centre front | 9 cm (3½") |
| Length of inside leg | 3.5 cm (1½") |

### Tension
16 sts in width, 16 rows in depth over 2.5 cm (1")

Instructions for smaller garments are given inside square brackets [].

See page 10 for abbreviations.

## Jumper

Knitted in one piece.
Starting at the back, with 3.75 mm (9) (US 5) [3 mm (11) (US 3)] needles and main colour wool, cast on 40 sts, and work in rib of k2, p2 for 5 rows.
*6th row:* Using contrast, knit 1 row
*7th row:* *k2, p2, repeat from *to end of row. Break off contrast.
*8th row:* Using main colour, knit 1 row, and then work 3 rows in k2, p2 rib.
Work 32 rows in garter st.
Cast on 12 sts at beginning of next row, knit across the 40 sts of back and cast on 12 more sts (for the sleeves).
Knit 7 rows.
*Next row:* Knit 32 sts, turn and knit backward and forward on these 32 sts for 7 rows, finishing at inside (neck) edge.
Cast off 12 sts (centre back), and knit the remaining 20 sts.
On these 20 sts work 22 rows (11 ribs). Break off wool, and leave these sts on spare needle.
Rejoin wool at neck edge of original part, and work other side to correspond, ending at neck edge.
Cast on 24 sts for front of neck, then knit the 20 sts from the spare needle (64 sts).
Knit 15 rows across the full width of garment.
Cast off 12 sts at beginning of next 2 rows (40 sts).
Knit 32 rows (16 ribs).
With right side of work facing you, work 4 rows of k2, p2 rib.
Rejoin contrast and knit one row.
*Next row:* k2, p2. Break off contrast.
With main colour, knit one row, and then work 4 rows of k2, p2 rib. Cast off.

*Cuffs*

With right side of work facing, pick up 28 sts at cuff edge, and with main colour work in k2, p2 rib for 3 rows.

Change to contrast, knit 1 row, and work next row in k2, p2 rib.

Change to main colour, knit 1 row, and work 3 rows in k2, p2 rib. Cast off.

Sew up side and sleeve seams.

*Neck*

*1st row:* Beginning at top of neck opening with 3.5 mm (9 or 10) (US E) [3 mm (11) (US D)] crochet hook and main colour, work loosely in treble (US dc) all around neck to other side of neck opening, working 3 sts tog at all the 4 corners.

*2nd row:* Work 1 row of double crochet (US sc), finishing down one side of the opening. Break off thread.

*3rd row:* With contrast, begin at top of work and work 1 row of treble (US dc), to other side, working 3 sts together at corners. Do not work down opening. Break off wool.

*4th row:* With main colour work double crochet (US sc) up side of opening, around neck (3 sts tog at corners), but do not work down other side of opening, turn.

*5th row:* Working quite loosely so that neck will stretch when pulling garment over doll's head, work 1 dc (US sc) into each previous dc (3 tog at corners), and work right down opening. End off.

One side of opening goes under the other. Sew on snap fasteners (press-studs) to close.

# Pants

With main colour and 3 mm (11) (US 3) [2.25 mm (13) (US 1)] needles, cast on 44 sts, and work 2 rows of k2, p2 rib.

*3rd row:* k1, *wool over needle, k2 tog, repeat from * to end, finishing with k1.

Work 3 rows in k2, p2 rib.

Change to 3.75 mm (9) (US 5) [3 mm (11) (US 3)] needles and knit one row.

*8th row:* Knit 6, turn and work back.

*Next row:* Knit 12, turn and work back.

*Next row:* Knit 18, turn and work back.

Continue in this way, knitting 6 more sts each time, until 8 sts are left. Knit to end.

Knit backward and forward across work for 10 rows (5 ribs).

Inc at the beginning of next row, and every following 4th row, until you have 48 sts on the needle. (*Note:* The side with the inc will be the back seam.)

Work in garter st for 14 rows (7 ribs).

Knit 2 tog at the beginning of each row, until you have only 40 sts.

Work 5 rows in k2, p2 rib. Cast off.

Work other leg exactly the same.

Carefully sew up the back seam (matching ribs formed by knitting) from top to start of dec st, then sew the front seam, and lastly sew the leg seams.

Run narrow elastic through holes at waist.

# *Bruce*  *illustrated on page 18*

This three-piece boy's outfit was designed some time before 1910. With a little variation it is completely at home on a 25–30 cm (10"–12") antique or reproduction doll on a kid body, or on a much later 35.5 cm (14") hard plastic doll of the 1950s–1960s era. With the legs worked a little longer it will suit a doll from any period.

## LARGER DOLL

### Materials
50 g (2 oz) 3-ply Bendigo fingering wool
Set of 4 double-pointed 3 mm (11) (US 3) needles
4 gold buttons for hat
2 small buttons for jumper
4 buttons for trouser legs (optional)

### Measurements
| | |
|---|---|
| *Jumper* Length from top of shoulder | 14 cm (5½") |
| Width around at underarm | 21 cm (8½") |
| Length of sleeve seam | 10 cm (4") |
| *Trousers* Length at centre front | 9 cm (3½") |
| Length of inside leg | 8 cm (3¼") |
| *Hat* Circumference (unstretched) | 22 cm (8½") |

### Tension
7 sts in width, 10 rows in depth over 2.5 cm (1") of smooth fabric.

## SMALLER DOLL

### Materials
25 g (1 oz) 2-ply fingering wool
Set of 4 double-pointed 2 mm (14) (US 0) needles
4 gold buttons for hat
2 small buttons or beads for jumper
4 buttons for trouser legs (optional)

### Measurements
| | |
|---|---|
| *Jumper* Length from top of shoulder | 10 cm (4") |
| Width around at underarm | 15.5 cm (6¼") |
| Length of sleeve seam | 6.5 cm (2½") |
| *Trousers* Length at centre front | 6 cm (2¼") |
| Length of inside leg | 6.5 cm (2½") |
| *Hat* Circumference unstretched | 12.5 cm (5") |

### Tension
11 sts in width, 16 rows in depth over 2.5 cm (1") of smooth fabric

Instructions for smaller garments are given in square brackets [].

See page 10 for abbreviations.

## Jumper

Using set of 3 mm (11) (US 3) [2 mm (14) (US 0)] needles, cast on 60 sts, with 30 sts on one needle and 15 each on the other two needles. The needle with 30 sts is referred to as the front needle, and the other two make up the back.
Work 8 rounds in k2, p2 rib.
Knit 32 rounds, purling the 30th and 60th sts on each round. This gives definition for the side seams, coming under each armhole.
Working on the front needle only, work in stocking st for 16 rows.
Cast off 3 sts at the beginning of the next four rows (the shoulders). Break off wool.
Place the remaining 18 sts on a spare needle.
Rejoin wool to the other sts, placing them all on one needle, and work 16 rows in stocking st for back.
Cast off 3 sts at the beginning of the next 4 rows.
Place the remaining 18 sts and the 18 sts from the spare needle on one needle and work loosely in k2, p2 rib for 4 rows. Cast off loosely in rib for neck.

*Sleeves*
Pick up 15 sts down each side of armhole, placing 10 sts on each needle, and knit 32 rows, decreasing 2 sts in the 10th and 20th rows.
Work 6 rows of k2, p2 rib. Cast off loosely in rib.

*To make up*
Sew up shoulder seam already joined at the neck. Fasten the other shoulder with 2 small buttons or beads.

# Pants

Cast on 48 sts, i.e. 16 sts on each of 3 needles, using 3 mm (11) (US 3) [2 mm (14) (US 0)] and work in k2, p2 rib for 6 rows.
Knit 24 rounds.
Place 24 sts onto a large safety pin.
Cast on 8 sts, and knit these with the other 24 sts for 32 rounds or length desired.
Early dolls wore knickerbockers (trousers to the knee), the length given in this pattern, but you may like to have the trousers shorter or longer.
Work 6 rows in k2, p2 rib. Cast off loosely in rib.
Rejoin wool to the 24 sts, and then knit into the back of the 8 cast-on sts to make the number equal for the second leg.
Knit 2nd leg to correspond with 1st leg and cast off.
If this garment is for an old doll or a reproduction of an old doll, sew two fancy buttons onto the outer side of each leg at the knee as a finishing touch.

# Cap

Cast on 52 sts, i.e. 18, 18 and 16, on the three 3 mm (11) (US 3) [2 mm (14) (US 0)] needles.
Work in k2, p2 rib for 6 rounds.
Knit 32 rounds.
Divide the sts equally onto two needles (26 on each).
Turn inside out so that the wrong side of work is now facing you.
Place the two needles side by side, and cast off by knitting from both needles at the same time (i.e. work as though you are only casting off 26 sts).

*To make up*
Fasten each corner of cap down to top of ribbing, and finish off with small gold buttons as decoration.

# *Darryl* *illustrated on page 27*

This outfit of shirt, pants, shoes and socks is particularly suitable for a 36 cm (14") hard plastic boy doll or composition doll of the 1940s or 1950s, although it can easily be worn by dolls of other eras. If you wish to make this outfit for a bigger doll, use thicker wools and bigger needles. See page 6 on changing the size of garments to suit different sized dolls.

## Materials

25 g (1 oz) Bendigo 2-ply fingering wool in white for the shirt and socks
25 g (1 oz) Bendigo 3-ply fingering wool in suitable colour for the pants and shoes
Pair 2.25 mm (13) (US 1) needles for the shirt and pants
Set of 4 double-pointed needles, size 2 mm (14) (US 0) for the socks and shoes
4 small buttons for front of shirt
4 larger buttons to fasten pants to shirt
2 small fancy buckles for shoes

## Measurements

| | | |
|---|---|---|
| *Shirt* Length from top of shoulder | 11 cm (4¼") |
| Width round underarm of garment | 25 cm (10") |
| *Pants* Length of centre front | 7.5 cm (3") |
| *Shoes* Sole | 5 cm (2") |

## Tension

2-ply fingering wools: 10 sts in width, 13 rows in depth, over 2.5 cm (1") of smooth fabric;
3-ply fingering wool: 10 sts in width, 13 rows in depth, over 2.5 cm (1") of smooth fabric.

See page 10 for abbreviations.

# Shirt

*Back*
With 2.25 mm (13) (US 1) needles and 2-ply wool, cast on 44 sts, and work 8 rows in k1, p1 rib.
Work 22 rows in stocking st.
To shape armholes: Cast off 5 sts at the beginning of the next 2 rows, then dec 1 st at both ends of the next row (32 sts).
Work 9 rows in stocking stitch.

*Yoke*
(p5, p2 tog) 4 times, p4 (28 sts).
*1st row of pattern:* k1, *sl 1, k2, psso (knit slip st as you pass it over the point of the right-hand needle before taking it off needle); repeat from * to end.
*2nd row:* Purl.
Repeat the two rows of pattern three times.
To slope shoulders: Continuing in pattern, cast off 4 sts at the beginning of the next 2 rows, then cast off 3 sts at the beginning of the following 2 rows. Cast off the remaining sts.

*Right front*
Using 2-ply white wool and 2.25 mm (13) (US 1) needles, cast on 28 sts, and work in single rib with moss stitch border as follows:
*1st row:* (right side) (p1, k1) twice, for the border, then (k1, p1) to end of row.
*2nd row:* *k1, p1, repeat from * to end of row.
Repeat these 2 rows three times.
*1st row:* (p1, k1) twice, k1, sl 1, k2, psso (knitting slip stitch as you pass it over point of right-hand needle). Knit to end.
*2nd row:* Purl to last 4 sts, k1, p1 twice.
Repeat the last two pattern rows 10 times, and the first row of pattern once.
To shape armhole: Cast off 5 sts at the beginning (armhole end) of the next row, then dec 1 st at armhole end on the following purl row (22 sts).
Work 2 rows in pattern.

*Yoke*
(Inc row) (p1, k1) twice, *k4, inc, repeat from * twice, knit to last st, inc (26 sts).
*1st row:* Purl to last 4 sts, (k1, p1) twice.
*2nd row:* (p1, k1) twice, k1, *sl 1, k2, psso (knitting slip

**ANTHONY** The two versions of this simple 1930s outfit are worn by dolls made on opposite sides of the globe. On the left a 46 cm (18") Armand Marseille 352/4 bisque china head on an Australian cloth body with celluloid arms and legs, manufactured by Laurie Cohen, Sydney; the smaller doll is a delightful 32 cm (12½") 'Baby Blue Eyes' celluloid baby doll, manufactured in Japan (circa 1937), holding a Victorian era tin rattle with wooden whistle. Pattern on page 12.

st as you pass it over point of right-hand needle), repeat from * to end.

Repeat these two pattern rows 3 times, and then 1st row again.

To shape neck:

*1st row:* Cast off 11 sts and work in pattern to end.

Continue in pattern, and dec 1 st at neck edge in the next 6 rows (8 sts).

To slope shoulder:

Cast off 4 sts at the beginning (armhole end) the next row. Work 1 row straight, then cast off remaining sts.

*Left front*

With 2-ply wool and using 2.25 mm (13) (US 1) needles, cast on 28 sts and work in rib with a moss stitch border as follows:

*1st row:* (right side) (p1, k1) to last 4 sts, (k1, p1) twice.

*2nd row:* *p1, k1, repeat from * to end of row.

Repeat these last 2 rows 3 times.

*1st row:* k20, sl 1, k2, psso, (knitting sl st as you pass it over the point of the right-hand needle), k1, (k1, p1) twice.

*2nd row:* (p1, k1) twice, purl to end.

Repeat these 2 pattern rows 10 times.

To shape armhole:

Cast off 5 sts, knit to last 8 sts, sl 1, k2, psso (as before), k1, (k1, p1) twice.

*2nd row:* (p1, k1) twice, purl to end.

*3rd row:* k2 tog, knit to last 8 sts, sl 1, k2, psso (as before), k1, (k1, p1) twice.

Repeat 2nd row (22 sts).

*Yoke*

(Inc row) k1, inc, (k3, inc) three times, sl 1, k2, psso (as before), k1, (k1, p1) twice (26 sts).

*1st row:* (p1, k1) twice, purl to end.

*2nd row:* k1, *sl 1, k2, psso (as before), repeat from * to last 5 sts, k1, (k1, p1) twice.

Repeat 1st and 2nd rows 4 times.

To shape neck:

Cast off 11 sts, continue in pattern to end.

Continuing in pattern dec 1 st at neck edge in the next 6 rows.

Slope shoulder as given for right front.

*Sleeves* (two alike)

Using 2-ply wool and 2.25 mm (12) (US 1) needles, cast on 36 sts and work 6 rows in k1, p1 rib.

Work 8 rows in stocking st.

To shape sleeve:

Cast off 4 sts at beg of next 2 rows, then dec 1 st at both ends of the next 8 rows. Cast off remaining sts.

*Collar*

With 2.25 mm (13) (US 1) needles and 2-ply wool, cast on 60 sts and work 3 rows in stocking st.

Continue in st st, but dec 1 st at each end of the next 4 rows (52 sts). Cast off loosely.

*To make up*

Press following instructions on page 6. Join shoulder seams, set sleeves into armholes and then join sleeve and side seams. Beginning and ending at inside edge of moss stitch, sew the cast-off edge of collar (easing to fit) to neck edge. Sew 4 small buttons to right side, and ease apart moss stitches on left side to fasten.

# Pants

*Right leg*

Beginning at the waist, cast on 44 sts with 3-ply wool and 2.25 mm (13) (US 1) needles, and work 3 rows in k1, p1 rib.

*Buttonhole row 1:* Rib 9, cast off 2 sts, rib 21, cast off 2 sts, rib 8.

*Buttonhole row 2:* Rib 9, cast on 2 sts (over cast-off sts), rib 22, cast on 2 sts, rib 9.

Work 3 more rows in k1, p1 rib.

To shape back:

k12, turn, and purl back.

*Next row:* k22, turn and purl back.

**Work 8 rows in st st across all sts.

Inc 1 st at each end of next row, and every following 4th row, until there are 52 sts on the needle.

Work 3 rows straight in st st.

Shape legs by casting off 2 sts at beginning of next 2 rows, and then dec 1 st at each end of the next 2 rows (44 sts).

Work 3 rows in rib, and cast off in rib.**

*Left leg*

Work the first 3 rows of rib, the 2 buttonhole rows, and the next 3 rows of rib as for the right leg, then proceed for shaping as follows:

Knit 1 row.

*1st row:* P12, turn and knit to end.

*Next row:* p22, turn and knit to end.

Work from ** to ** as for right leg.

---

**BRUCE**   Standing beside the lovely miniature chest of drawers made on a 1:6 scale by Jim Fainges are two dolls wearing their Bruce outfits. The larger doll, a hard plastic boy doll with moulded hair, stands 35.5 cm (14") tall, and was manufactured by Pedigree England in the 1950s–1960s. The smaller doll, 28 cm (11") tall, is a character Heubach made in Germany in the early years of this century. The doll has a bisque porcelain head, intaglio eyes and a kid body. Pattern on page 14.

*To make up*
Press as for shirt, then join the centre front and back seams, then the leg seams. Button pants onto waist ribbing of shirt.

# Shoes (two alike)

With two 2 mm (14) (US 0) needles and 3-ply wool, cast on 6 sts.

*The sole*
*1st row:* knit.
*2nd row:* Inc, purl to last st, inc.
Repeat these 2 rows twice (12 sts).
Work 16 rows in st st, then dec 1 st at each end of the next 2 rows (8 sts).

*Upper shoe*
*1st row:* Inc, k to last st, inc.
*2nd row:* Purl.
Repeat last 2 rows 4 times (18 sts).
*Next row:* k7, cast off 4, knit to end.
*Side:*
On last 7 sts work as follows:
Purl 1 row.
*Next row:* sl 1, k1, psso, k5.
Work 13 rows in st st on these 6 sts. Cast off.
Rejoin wool to the wrong side of remaining 7 sts and work thus:
*1st row:* p 7.
*2nd row:* k5, k2 tog.
Work 13 rows in st st, then cast off.
Join back seam, and sew upper part of shoe to sole. Finish off by placing a fancy buckle on top of instep of each shoe. If you wish you may work one row of double crochet (US sc) all round instep.

# Socks

Using white 2-ply wool and a set of four 2 mm (14) (US 0) needles, cast on 32 sts (12, 10, 10, over the three needles).
Work 6 rounds in moss stitch (k1, p1).
Knit 10 rounds.
*Next row:* k12, then k4 from 2nd needle, and work on these 16 sts for the heel flap, leaving the remaining 16 sts on two needles until required to work the instep.

*Heel flap*
Work 7 rows in stocking st, beginning with a purl row.
Turning the heel:
*1st row:* k9, sl 1, k1, psso, k1, turn.
*2nd row:* sl 1, p3, p2 tog, p1, turn.
*3rd row:* sl 1, k4, sl 1, k1, psso, k1, turn.
*4th row:* sl 1, p5, p2 tog, p1, turn.
*5th row:* sl 1, k6, sl 1, k1, psso, k1, turn.
*6th row:* sl 1, p7, p2 tog, p1, turn (10 sts).
*Next row:* k10, pick up and knit 8 sts from the side edge of the heel flap; with 2nd needle knit along the next 16 sts for the instep, then with 3rd needle pick up and knit 8 sts from the side edge at the opposite side of the heel flap. K5 from 1st needle onto 3rd needle (42 sts all round).
Knit one round.
*Dec round:*
   *On 1st needle, k until 2 sts remain, k2 tog.
   On 2nd needle, k.
   On 3rd needle, sl 1, k1, psso, k to end.*
Repeat from * to * 4 times (32 sts).
Work 6 rounds without decreasing.
To shape the toe:
*1st dec round:*
   On 1st needle, k until 2 sts remain, k2 tog.
   On 2nd needle, sl 1, k1, psso, k until 2 sts remain, k2 tog.
   On 3rd needle, sl 1, k1, psso, k to end.
Repeat the last round, 3 times.
*Next round:* k4 sts from the 1st needle onto the 3rd needle. You now have 8 sts on each of 2 needles. Place the 2 needles side by side, and cast off the 16 sts together as if they were only 8 sts.
Fasten off securely. Work another sock the same way.

# *David* *illustrated on page 27*

Really simple to make, this very attractive romper suit is ideal for a 40–46 cm (16"–18") celluloid or composition doll of the 1920s–1930s period, but is equally suited to other dolls of a different period. The pattern has been adapted from the 1932 book *Dress your Dolly in Knitting and Crochet* by Ella Allan.

## Materials

50 g (2 oz) Bendigo 3-ply fingering wool in white or other main colour
Small ball contrast 3-ply wool
Pair 4 mm (8) (US 6) knitting needles
Pair 2.75 mm (12) (US 2) knitting needles
2 press-studs (snap fasteners)
Other materials may be used, but the garment may not finish up the same size.

## Measurements

| | |
|---|---|
| From top of shoulder to bottom of leg ribbing | 25.5 cm (10") |
| From bottom of neck ribbing to front crutch | 20.5 cm (8") |
| Width around at underarm | 33 cm (13") |
| (As this is a stretchy knit, this garment can fit a doll with a larger girth) | |
| Length of inside leg seam | 5 cm (2") |
| Length of sleeve from underarm | 6 cm (2½") |
| Length of belt | 28 cm (11") |

## Tension

12 sts in width, 12 rows in depth over 2.5 cm (1").

See page 10 for abbreviations.

## Back (one piece)

With 2.75 mm (12) (US 2) needles and white wool, cast on 28 sts (back of neck).
*1st row:* *k2, p2, repeat from * to end of row.
*2nd, 3rd and 4th rows:* Repeat 1st row.
*5th row:* (join in contrast), knit.
*6th row:* *k2, p2, repeat from * to end of row (break off contrast).
*7th row:* (with white wool), knit.
*8th row:* Repeat 1st row (break off wool to darn in later).
Using 4 mm (8) (US 6) needles, and white wool, cast on 6 sts and knit 3 rows.
*Next row:* Knit across ribbing from spare needle, and cast on 6 sts at other end of needle (40 sts).

Work 52 rows in garter st (26 ribs) to waistline.
*1st row* (of pants section): k24, turn.
Knit 8, turn.
Knit 16, turn.
Knit 24, turn.
Continue in this way, knitting 8 sts more each time until all stitches are knitted (40 sts).
Work in garter st for 44 rows (22 ribs).

Leg shaping:
** Beginning at edge of work, k18, k2 tog, turn and knit back.
*Next row:* k17, k2 tog, turn and knit back.
*Next row:* k16, k2 tog, turn and knit back.
*Next row:* k15, k2 tog.
Change to 2.75 mm (12) (US 2) needles and work 5 rows of k2, p2 rib. Cast off.**
Rejoin wool to body of rompers, and work other side of leg from ** to **.

## Front (one piece)

With 2.75 mm (12) (US 2) needles, work the first 8 rows of ribbing as given for back.
With white wool and 4 mm (8) (US 6) needles, cast on 6 sts, knit across the 28 rib sts and then cast on 6 more sts (40 sts).
Work in garter st for 96 rows (48 ribs).
Finish off legs by knitting the same as back from ** to ** on both sides of romper front.
Sew right shoulder seam.
Sew edge of left shoulder together.

*Sleeves*
With 4 mm (8) (US 6) needles cast on 28 sts and work in garter st for 20 rows (10 ribs).
Change to 2.75 mm (12) (US 2) needles and work 2 rows in k2, p2 ribbing.
Join in contrast, knit 1 row, then work 1 row in k2, p2 rib.
Change to main colour, knit 1 row, and then work 3 rows in k2, p2 ribbing. Cast off.
Work another sleeve the same.

*To make up*
Mark middle of sleeve, and gently stretching, sew sleeves in place, with middle of sleeve matching shoulder seams. Sew up rest of side seam, and sleeve seam. Sew up inside leg seams. Sew press-stud at left side of neck and shoulder.

# Belt

With 4 mm (8) (US 6) needles and white wool, cast on 60 sts, and knit 2 rows.
Join in contrast and knit 2 rows. Break off thread.
With white wool knit 2 rows. Cast off. Darn in ends.
Sew a snap fastener (press-stud) to join ends of belt at back when placed around waist.
As an alternative, place a small fancy buckle in the middle on right side of belt, which will then be worn at the front of rompers.

# *Edward* illustrated on page 28

A wonderful outfit for both dolls and bears. Probably the simplest outfit in the book, and yet so elegant, this classic suit for a boy doll or a teddy bear has been adapted from a pattern produced some time between 1910 and 1920. The unusual part of this outfit is that it is based on a series of rectangles, entirely knitted in garter stitch, so it can be knitted by anyone who is capable of knitting, and can be worn by any doll or bear regardless of age. The shoes are the only part not made from a rectangle.

## Materials

75 g (3 oz) Bendigo 3-ply fingering wool
Small amount of contrast if required for edging, but outfit is equally elegant without
Pair 3.25 mm (10) (US 3) needles
Pair 2.75 mm (12) (US 2) needles (for the shoes)
Medium sized crochet hook to work the contrast crochet edging
6 gold buttons for the jacket
2 small buttons for the shoes
Small gold buckle (if you wish to use the belt)
Length of elastic for the pants

## Measurements

(Garter st is a marvellous st which stretches.)

| | |
|---|---|
| *Jacket* Length from shoulder to hem | 12 cm (5") |
| Width from front edge to front edge at underarm | 28 cm (11") |
| Length of sleeve to underarm | 9 cm (3½") |
| Length of belt | 28 cm (11") |
| *Trousers* Length of front seam | 8 cm (3¼") |
| Length of inside leg seam | 6 cm (2½") |
| *Hat* Circumference (unstretched) | 28 cm (11") |
| *Shoe* Sole of foot | 5 cm (2") |

## Tension

12 sts in width, 14 rows in depth, over 2.5 cm (1").

See page 10 for abbreviations.

## Trousers (two rectangles)

*Leg*
With 3.25 mm (10) (US 3) needles cast on 30 sts and work 60 rows in garter st (30 ribs). Cast off.
Work another piece the same for the other leg.

*To make up*
Place the two pieces together, matching ribs. For the front seam, sew down from the cast-off edges of both pieces for 15 ribs, being careful to match as you sew.
Repeat for back seam. The pants have now been formed, but the bottoms of the legs aren't sewn, so keeping the knitted ribs matching, sew up the two leg seams (that is 15 ribs for each leg).
With a medium crochet hook, work one row of double crochet (US sc) around the bottom of each leg (this may be done in the contrast colour).
For the waist, work one row of treble crochet (US dc) around the top of the trousers. Fasten off.
Run a length of elastic through the trebles.

## Jacket

(Made up of 6 rectangles, plus two pockets and one belt if desired)

*Back*
With 3.25 mm (10) (US 3) needles, cast on 28 sts and work 56 rows in garter st (28 ribs). Cast off.

*Fronts*
Cast on 22 sts and work 56 rows in garter st (28 ribs). Cast off. Knit another rectangle for the other front.

*Sleeves*
Cast on 35 sts, and work 40 rows in garter st (20 ribs). Cast off. Knit another rectangle for the other sleeve.

*Collar*
Cast on 12 sts, and work 80 rows in garter st (40 ribs). Cast off.

*Pockets*
Cast on 10 sts, and work 12 rows in garter st (6 ribs). Cast off. Work another piece the same.

*Belt*
Cast on 80 sts, work 5 rows in garter st. Cast off.

*To make up jacket*

Matching ribs, sew up 17 ribs of one front piece to one side of the back. Sew up the second front to the other side of the back for 17 ribs. With cast-off edges of the fronts and back matching, sew across 7 sts on each side of the top edge of back and fronts for the shoulder seam. Sew up side seams of both sleeves, making sure you match the ribs as before. Pin in place in armhole with side seam of sleeve and jacket matching, and sew neatly into armhole. Fold the collar and back of jacket in half, and mark each with a pin. Sew collar to jacket, matching pins, but starting and ending collar a little back from the front edges to form a lapel when front of jacket is folded over.

Work a row of double crochet (US sc) all around edge of jacket (in contrast if you desire), working three loops of chain st on edge of one front to serve as buttonholes. Sew three buttons to match buttonholes on other side, and sew three other buttons to correspond to give a double-breasted look if the doll or bear is thin enough. Work one row of double crochet (US sc) on the edge of the sleeves, the pockets and, if you wish, the belt (I prefer it plain). Sew pockets in place on jacket.

# Cap

With 3.25 mm (10) (US 3) needles cast on 56 sts and work 48 rows in garter st (24 ribs).

Matching the ribs, join up the back seam. Work 1 row of double crochet (US sc) around the cast-on edge, and gather the other edge in tightly with matching wool. If you wish sew a matching pompom on top.

*Tuft or simple pompom*

Wind double wool 20 times around four fingers, slip off and tie firmly in the middle; cut through the loops and trim the ends to form a round ball.

# Shoes

Using 2.75 mm (13) (US 2) needles, cast on 21 sts.
Knit 1 row.
*1st row:* k1, inc in next st, k7, inc in next st, k1, inc in next st, k7, inc in next st, k1.
*2nd and alternate rows:* Knit.
*3rd row:* k1, inc in next st, k9, inc in next st, k1, inc in next st, k9, inc in next st, k1.
*5th row:* k1, inc in next st, k11, inc in next st, k1, inc in next st, k11, inc in next st, k1.
*7th row:* k1, inc in next st, k13, inc in next st, k1, inc in next st, k13, inc in next st, k1.
Work 5 rows in garter st.
*Next row:* k22, k2 tog, turn, then:
*sl 1, k8, k2 tog*.
Repeat from * to * until 28 sts remain.
Knit right across the needle. Cast off.
Sew up back seam and sole of foot.

*Strap*

Cast on 15 sts, pick up and knit 3 sts on each side of the back seam, cast on 15 sts (36 sts).
Knit 1 row through back of sts.
*Next row:* k2, wl fwd, k2 tog, knit to end.
*Next row:* Knit. Cast off.
Work another shoe the same way, working buttonhole in strap thus:
Knit to last three sts, wl fwd, k2 tog, k1.
Sew a small button on strap, so that the shoe can button up around the ankle.

As I remarked at the beginning, what outfit could be simpler, yet so elegant, for a bear or a boy doll? You can make it in any colour or combination of colours that you wish. Should you want to make the outfit for a bigger doll or bear, just increase the ply of the wool and the size of the needles, e.g. 4-ply wool and 3.75 mm (9) (US 5) needles or 5-ply wool and 4 mm (8) (US 6) needles, and so on. The same applies if you wish to make the outfit smaller—just reduce the ply and the size of the needle in proportion.

Most of these outfits are equally suited to bears.

# *Geoffrey*  *illustrated on page 39*

A three-piece outfit, comprising jumper, pants and cap, suitable for any of the 16.5 cm (6½") hard plastic dolls which were so popular in the 1950s and 1960s. The outfit is also suitable as a modern track suit for the small vinyl dolls so easily available today.

## Materials
25 g (1 oz) Bendigo 2-ply fingering wool in MC
25 g (1 oz) Bendigo 2-ply fingering wool in C
(For a modern vinyl doll you could substitute 3-ply nylon baby wool; the two yarns are similar in thickness, and knit up to practically the same size.)
Pair 2 mm (14) (US 0) knitting needles
Small press-stud
Length of hat elastic

## Measurements
| | |
|---|---|
| *Jumper* From top of shoulder | 7 cm (2¾") |
| Width around underarm | 13 cm (5") |
| *Pants* Length of front seam | 4.5 cm (1¾") |
| Length of inside leg | 5 cm (2") |
| *Cap* To fit head circumference | 11 cm (4½") |

## Tension
10 sts in width, 14 rows in depth over 2.5 cm (1") smooth fabric.

See page 10 for abbreviations.

## Pants

Begin at the waist with 2-ply in main colour. Using 2 mm (14) (US 0) needles, cast on 26 sts.
Work 6 rows in k1, p1 rib.
Work 11 rows in stocking st, ending with a purl row.
Inc 1 st at each end of the next row (28 sts).
Cast on 3 sts at beginning of the next 2 rows, and work 4 rows in st st (34 sts).
Dec 1 st at each end of the next row and following 4th row 4 times; work 3 rows (24 sts).
*Next row:* *k3, k2 tog*, 4 times, k4 (20 sts).
Work 4 rows in k1, p1 rib. Cast off.
Work a second leg the same way.
Join up centre back and front seams, then leg seams. Thread hat elastic through the waist ribbing.

## Jumper

With 2-ply wool in MC, and 2 mm (14) (US 0) needles, cast on 24 sts.
Work 8 rows in k1, p1 rib. (Carry the threads of the two colours up side of garment.)
Join in contrast (C).
*1st row:* Knit.
*2nd row:* Purl.
*3rd row:* MC, knit.
*4th row:* MC, purl.
Repeat the last 4 rows 4 times, and the first 2 rows once.
To shape the neck:
K8 for left shoulder, turn; keeping continuity of pattern, work 6 rows. Cast off.
Rejoin wool, cast off 8 sts for neck, k8, and repeat as for left shoulder.

*Back*
With MC cast on 24 sts. Work 8 rows in rib, and then 20 rows in stripe pattern (as for front).
*Next row:* k12, cast on 2 sts (back opening).
*1st row:* k2, p12.
*2nd row:* k14.
Keeping continuity of stripe pattern, and with garter st border at centre back, work 5 rows.
Cast off 6 sts (neck). Work 2 rows, cast off remaining sts.
Rejoin wool, cast on 2 sts, k12.
*1st row:* p12, k2.
*2nd row:* k14.
Keeping continuity of stripe pattern, and with garter st border at centre back, work 4 rows.
Cast off 6 sts for neck. Work 2 rows. Cast off remaining sts.

*Sleeves*
With MC and 2 mm (14) (US 0) needles, cast on 16 sts and work 4 rows in rib.
Join in C, and work pattern as for front; keeping continuity of pattern, inc 1 st at both ends of the 5th row, and every following 6th row twice.
Work 3 rows, and cast off.
Work another sleeve the same.

*Neck*

With right side of work facing, and using MC and 2 mm (14) (US 0) needles, begin just inside the garter st border at the left side of back opening. Pick up and knit 13 sts from the neck edge of the left back and shoulder, pick up and knit 8 sts across front neck, and then pick up and knit 13 sts from neck edge of right shoulder and back, finishing just inside the garter st border (34 sts).

Work 6 rows in k1, p1 rib. Cast off.

*To make up*

Press following instructions on page 6. Catch left side of back opening to base of right side of back opening. Fold neck rib over and catch to inside of jumper.

Sew a small press-stud at back to close opening.

Join sleeve and side seams.

# Cap

With MC wool, and 2 mm (14) (US 0) needles, cast on 48 sts, and work 14 rows in k1, p1 rib.

Join in C and, following stripe pattern as set for front of jumper, work 12 rows.

To shape top:

*1st row:* *k4, k2 tog, repeat from * to end (40 sts).

*2nd row and all alternate rows:* Purl.

*3rd row:* *k3, k2 tog, repeat from * to end.

*5th row:* *k2, k2 tog, repeat from * to end.

*7th row:* *k1, k2 tog, repeat from * to end.

*8th row:* Purl.

Break off wool, thread through remaining sts, draw up tight and end off.

*To make up*

Sew up seam, and fold back half of ribbing.

---

*Opposite (left):* **DARRYL**   A 36 cm (14") hard plastic Roddy walking doll, made in England in the 1950s–1960s, stands beside a pressed metal Triang truck, made in England in the same period. Pattern on page 16.

*Opposite (right):* **DAVID**   Wearing an outfit designed in the 1920s–1930s period, quite a few years before the doll was made in Poland, this lovely 49 cm (19") celluloid doll is holding a felt koala bear designed and made by Marjory. Pattern on page 21.

*Page 28:* **EDWARD**   Like all the patterns in this book, this outfit is just as much at home on a doll as on a bear. The doll is a 41 cm (16") hard plastic Cherub walking doll, manufactured in Victoria in the 1950s. The 30.5 cm (12") teddy bear, wearing exactly the same outfit, is an original 'Miffi' bear, created and crafted by Marjory. Pattern on page 23.

*Page 29:* **KENNETH**   Many 25–28 cm (10"–11") dolls made of hard plastic were manufactured by various companies throughout the world. This unusual little doll, with his Roddy-like arms and legs, carries the Moldex logo in the middle of his back. He was made in Melbourne in the 1950s. Kenneth loves to play with his pre-1940s excelsior-filled white and tan fur dog with glass eyes. Pattern on page 33.

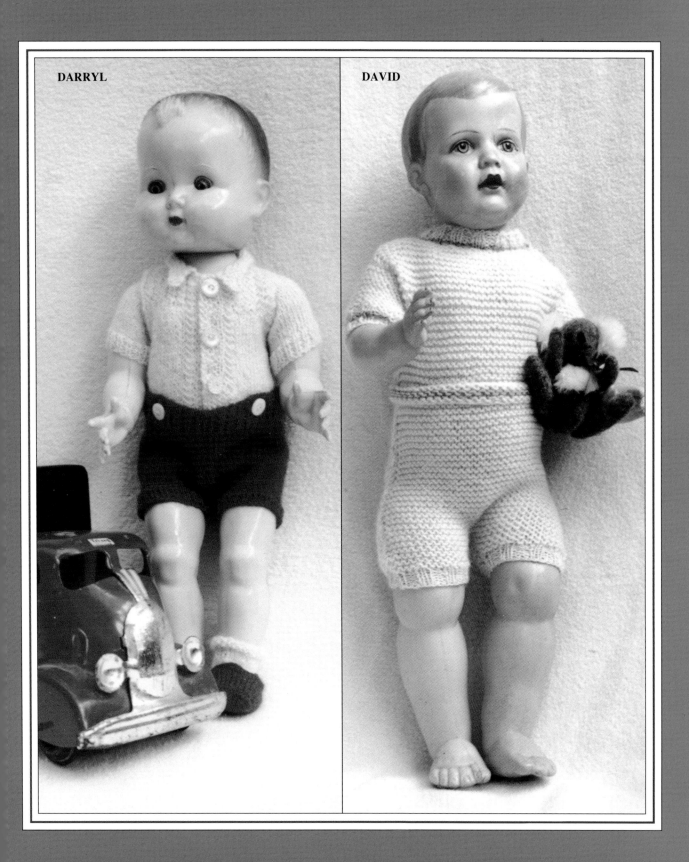

DARRYL

DAVID

27

KENNETH

# *Jack Tar* *illustrated opposite*

Coats Patons have kindly given permission for the reproduction of this sailor suit from Patons Knitting Book No. 252. The pattern, which consists of a jacket, trousers and cap, was originally designated 'Sally Sailor'; it would be suitable for a cloth-bodied doll of the 1940s or 1950s, but is also suitable for other 41 cm (16") slender dolls. As this pattern is very easily adapted and altered for length, measure the doll you wish to dress, and alter the length in the areas mentioned in the pattern, remembering that more navy wool will be required for longer garments.

## Materials
50 g (2 oz) 4-ply Patonyle in navy or other suitable colour
50 g (2 oz) 4-ply Patonyle in white
Pair 3.25 mm (10) (US 3) knitting needles
Pair 2.75 mm (12) (US 2) knitting needles
2.25 mm (13) (US B) crochet hook
Two press-studs
Length of elastic

## Measurements (to fit 41 cm (16") doll)

| | |
|---|---|
| *Jacket* Length from top of shoulder | 12 cm (4¾") |
| | (or length desired) |
| Width around at underarm | 25 cm (10") |
| Length of sleeve to underarm | 9.5 cm (3¾") |
| | (or length desired) |
| *Trousers* Length from waist to | 7.5 cm (3") |
| front crutch | (or length desired) |
| Length of inside leg seam | 15 cm (6") |
| | (or length desired) |
| *Cap:* To fit head circumference up to | 26 cm (10¼") |

## Tension
8 sts in width, 10 rows in depth over 2.5 cm (1") of smooth fabric.

See page 10 for abbreviations.

## Jacket

*Front*
Using 2.75 mm (12) (US 2) needles, and white wool, cast on 36 sts and work 2 cm (¾") in k1, p1 rib.

Change to 3.25 mm (10) (US 3) needles, and continue in stocking stitch until work measures 5 cm (2"). (If you wish to make the jacket longer, increase number of rows of stocking stitch here, remembering to increase the back to match.)
Shape armholes: Cast off 2 stitches at beginning of next 2 rows, then k2 tog at each end of next 2 rows.
Work straight until piece measures 8.5 cm (3¼") or length desired.
Shape neck:
*Next row:* k11, cast off 6 sts loosely, knit to end.
Continue on last 11 sts only, decreasing at neck edge in every row until 7 sts remain.
Work 4 rows straight, then cast off.
Work the other 11 sts to correspond.

*Back*
Work exactly as for front to completion of armhole shapings, then continue straight until length equals that of front to shoulders. Cast off straight across.

*Sleeves*
With 2.75 mm (12) (US 2) needles, and navy wool, cast on 22 stitches, and work 1.5 cm (½") in k1, p1 rib.
Change to 3.25 mm (10) (US 3) needles and white wool, and continue in stocking stitch, increasing at each end of 5th and every following 6th row until there are 30 sts on the needle.
Work straight until sleeve measures 9 cm (3½") or length desired.
Shape top:
Cast off 3 sts at beginning of next 2 rows, then k2 tog

**JACK TAR** A typical 41–46 cm (16"–18") wartime doll, having a composition head marked 'Plaitoy', with cloth arms and legs. Many dolls with composition heads resembling this doll were manufactured by various firms around the world. They were often unmarked, so this sailor outfit is excellent as a costume for such a doll. What sailor doll would be seen without his boat, even if it is a tin one made in Japan? Pattern on this page.

at each end of every row until 16 sts remain. Cast off loosely.

## Collar

With 3.25 mm (10) (US 3) needles, and navy wool, cast on 38 sts. Knit 7 rows in garter st, slipping the first stitch in every row (which gives a very neat edge). Continue in stocking st with border of 4 garter stitches at each side until work measures 5 cm (2").

*Next row:* k12, cast off 14 sts loosely, knit to end.

Work on last 12 sts only, keeping garter stitch border at outer edge, and decreasing at inside (neck) edge on every alternate row until 9 sts remain.

Now decrease on every 3rd row until 4 sts remain.

Continue in garter st for 2.5 cm (1"), then cast off.

Work remaining 12 sts to correspond.

## To make up

Catch shoulder seams together at armhole edges, then insert sleeves flat. Join side and sleeve seams in one. Fasten each shoulder with a press-stud, then stitch centre of collar along back of neck. In the navy wool make a crochet chain loop of 8 chain, stitch to front, and then slip ends of collar through loop.

# Trousers

Bellbottoms, with front and back alike.

With 3.25 mm (10) (US 3) needles and navy wool, cast on 23 sts for right front leg, and work 6 rows garter stitch.

Change to stocking st and decrease at beginning of every following 8th row (outside edge), until 18 sts remain.

Work straight until piece measures 15 cm (6") or length of leg desired, from start, ending with a purl row, then leave on a spare needle.

Make another piece to correspond for left front leg, reversing shapings, then join the two pieces together by working across all 36 stitches.

Continue in stocking stitch for another 6.5 cm (2½"), or length desired, then change to 2.75 mm (12) (US 2) needles, and work 3 rows in k1, p1 rib.

*Next row:* Make holes for elastic thus:

Rib 1, *wl fwd, rib 2 tog, repeat from * to last stitch, rib 1. Rib 2 more rows, then cast off in rib.

## Back

Work exactly the same as the fronts of trousers.

## To make up

Join leg and side seams, then thread elastic through holes at waist.

# Cap

(The cap is worked in crochet. American readers please refer to page 11 for translation of crochet terms.

For those who can't crochet, pick another beret included in this book and work in navy wool; unfortunately, it won't have quite the same effect.)

With navy wool and crochet hook make 4ch; join into ring with slip st then work 8 dc into ring.

*1st round:* 2ch, then 2 dc on each st (join with sc to top of 2ch at end of each round).

*2nd round:* 2ch, *2 dc on first st, 1 dc on next, repeat from * to end.

*3rd round:* 2ch, *2 dc on first st, 1 dc on each of next 2 sts, repeat from * to end.

*4th round:* 2ch, *2 dc on first st, 1 dc on each of next 3 sts, repeat from * to end.

*5th round:* 2ch, *2 dc on first st, 1 dc on each of next 4 sts, repeat from * to end.

Continue in this manner, working an extra st between increases each time, until 17th round is completed.

Decrease as follows:

*1st round:* 2ch, *miss 1 st, 17 dc, repeat from * to end.

*2nd round:* 2ch, *miss 1 st, 16 dc, repeat from * to end.

*3rd round:* 2ch, *miss 1 st, 15 dc, repeat from * to end.

Continue in this way, decreasing 1 st in each section in every row until 7 sts remain.

*Next round:* 1 dc on each stitch all round. Fasten off.

## To make up cap

If you wish, make a small white or red pompom and stitch to centre of crown. Work a suitable name in white wool on band at centre front.

# *Kenneth* *illustrated on page 29*

A lovely winter set of pointed cap, coat and leggings for a 28–31 cm (11"–12") baby boy doll, adapted from the December 9, 1939 *English Woman's Weekly*. If you want to be in keeping with the age of the pattern, the doll should be either a composition, celluloid or bisque (china) headed doll, but the clothes can equally well be worn by a 1950s or 1960s hard plastic doll, or even a small doll of today.

## Materials

50 g (2 oz) Bendigo 3-ply fingering wool (other materials may be used but the final result may not be the same)
Pair 3.25 mm (10) (US 3) knitting needles
4 small buttons
Length of hat elastic for the leggings
1 metre (1 yard) matching ribbon for the cap and the feet of the leggings

## Measurements

| | |
|---|---|
| *Jacket* Length from shoulder | 10 cm (4") |
| Width around at underarm | 25 cm (10") |
| Length of sleeve to underarm | 7 cm (2¾") |
| *Leggings* Length from waist to crutch | 6.5 cm (2½") |
| Length of inside leg to sole of foot | 11 cm (4¼") |
| *Cap* Length around face from neck edge | 18 cm (7") |

## Tension

9 sts in width, 11 rows in depth over 2.5 cm (1") of smooth fabric.

See page 10 for abbreviations.

## Coat

*Back*
Cast on 35 sts for lower edge and work 4 rows in garter st (working into back of sts on 1st row to give a neat edge).
Work 4 rows in st st, and then 4 rows in garter st.
Work 18 rows in st st to armholes.
To shape armholes:
Cast off 2 sts at the beginning of each of the next 2 rows, then dec 1 st at the beginning of each of the next 4 rows (27 sts).
Work 12 rows straight in st st and cast off.

*Left front*
Cast on 27 sts and work 4 rows in garter st (working into back of sts on first row).
*1st row:* Knit.
*2nd row:* k3, p3, k2, purl to end.
Repeat the last 2 rows once.

Knit 4 rows in garter st, and then the 2 pattern rows 5 times.
*Buttonhole row:* k23, k2 tog into the back of the sts, m1, k2.
Work the 2nd pattern row, then repeat the 2 pattern rows 3 times more to armhole.

To shape the armhole:
*1st row:* Cast off 2 sts, k20, k2 tog (through back of st), m1, k2.
*Next row:* k3, p3, k2, purl to end.
Continue in pattern, decreasing 1 st at the beginning (armhole end) of the next row and following alternate row (23 sts).
Work 2 pattern rows.
*Buttonhole row:* k18, k2 tog in back of stitch, m1, k2.
Work 2nd pattern row.

To shape neck:
**Cast off 9 sts at the beginning (neck edge) of the next row, then continue in st st, decreasing 1 st at the neck end of the next row and following 2 alt rows (11 sts).
Work 3 rows. Cast off.**

*Right front*
Cast on 27 sts and work 4 rows in garter st (working into back of stitches on first row), then begin pattern as follows:
*1st row:* Knit.
*2nd row:* Purl until 8 sts remain, k2, p3, k3.
Repeat these 2 rows once.
Work 4 rows in garter st, then work the 2 pattern rows 9 times, and the 1st row again.
To shape the armhole:
Cast off 2 sts at the beginning (armhole end) of the next row, work 1 row, then dec 1 st at the armhole end of the next row and following alt row (23 sts).
Work 4 pattern rows to the neck.
Continue from ** to ** of the left front to end.

*Sleeves*
Begin at the wrist and cast on 20 sts. Work 4 rows in garter st (working into back of stitches in first row).
Work 4 rows in st st.

33

Repeat the last 8 rows once more, then continue in st st, inc 1 st at each end of the next row and two following 6th rows (26 sts).
Work 3 rows straight in st st.
To shape the sleeve top:
Dec 1 st at both ends of the next row and following 3 alternate rows. Cast off.

*Collar*
First join the shoulder seams, beginning at the armhole end. Sew by taking 1 st from each side at a time. Beginning at the 5th st from the edge on the right front, pick up and purl 27 sts from all round the neck edge, ending at the 5th st from opposite edge.
Work 2 rows in st st with k2 border at each end of the p row, then inc 2 sts just inside the k2 border at each end of the next row and on following 2 alternate rows.
Work 2 rows in garter st. Cast off.

*To make up*
First press all parts following instructions on page 6. Set the sleeves into the armholes, and then join sleeve and side seams in one line. Sew 4 buttons to the right front (2 on the border and 2 on the garter st stripe).

# Leggings

Begin at the waist edge of one leg and cast on 40 sts.
Work 6 rows in single rib, then work 20 rows in st st.
Continue in st st, dec 1 st at each end of the next row and following 7 alternate rows (24 sts).
Work 23 rows straight in st st.
*Slot row:* *k1, m1, k2 tog, repeat from * to end.
Work 5 rows in st st, then 6 rows in garter st. Cast off.
Work a second leg in the same way.
Press both legs. Join the centre front and back seams, then join the leg and underfoot seams. Thread ribbon through the slots and thread hat elastic between the ribs at the waist.

# Pointed cap

Begin at the neck edge of the left side, and cast on 20 sts.
Work 2 rows in garter st.
*Slot row:* k1, *m1, k2 tog, repeat from * until 1st remains, k1.
*Next row:* k3, p2, k2, purl to end.
Work in pattern as follows:
*1st row:* (right side) Knit.
*2nd row:* k3, p2, k2, purl to end.
Repeat these 2 rows once.
Continue in pattern and inc in the 2nd st from the beginning of the next row, and every following 4th row, until 8 inc rows have been worked and there are 28 sts.
Work 3 rows.
Shape for peak as follows:
** *Next 2 rows:* k6, turn, p6.
Work 2 rows in pattern, across all the sts.
*Next 2 rows:* k4, turn and purl 4.
Work 2 rows in pattern across all sts.
*Next 2 rows:* k2, turn and purl 2***.
Pattern 2 rows, then repeat from *** back to **.
Pattern 2 rows, then k tog the 2nd and 3rd st from the beginning of the next row, and every following 4th row (decreasing at the same edge as the increases) until 8 dec rows are worked and 20 sts remain.
Work 3 rows.
*Slot row:* k1, *m1, k2 tog, repeat from * until 1 st remains, k1.
Work 2 rows in garter st. Cast off.

*To make up*
Press work, then fold the cap in half and join the shaped edges for the back seam. Thread ribbon through slot holes at neck.

# Michael *illustrated on page 40*

A boy doll's legginette set, reproduced with permission of Coats Patons from their early knitting pattern book *Specialty Gift and Craft Book No. 43*, and adapted to today's knitting idioms. This book would have been in circulation before World War II. The ideal doll to dress in this outfit of cap, coat, leggings and shoes would be a 30–32 cm (12"–13") bisque (china) headed baby doll, a composition baby doll or small celluloid doll, but any doll of this size can also wear this delightful, yet so simple outfit.

## Materials

50 g (2 oz) Patons 3-ply baby wool
Pair 3.25 mm (10) (US 3) needles for the main garments
Pair 2.75 mm (12) (US 2) needles for the shoes
5 small buttons
Length of hat elastic
Should you wish to make this outfit in a bigger size, use Patonyle 4-ply fingering yarn with 4 mm (8) (US 5 or 6) needles for the main garments, and 3.25 mm (10) (US 3) needles for the shoes. In 5-ply the garments would be even larger, using 4.5 mm (7) (US 7) needles for the main garments and 3.75 mm (9) (US 5) needles for the shoes.

## Measurements

| | | |
|---|---|---|
| *Coat:* Length from top of shoulder | 13 cm | (5¼") |
| Width all round at underarm | 28 cm | (11") |
| Length of sleeve to underarm | 7.5 cm | (3") |
| | | (can be lengthened to suit) |
| *Leggings:* Length of front seam | 9 cm | (3½") |
| Length of inside leg seam | 9 cm | (3½") |
| *Cap:* To fit head circumference of | 26–30 cm | (10"–12") |
| *Shoes:* Sole of foot | 4 cm | (1½") |

## Tension

8½ sts in width, 10 rows in depth over 2.5 cm (1") of smooth fabric.

See page 10 for abbreviations

## Cap

Using 3.25 mm (10) (US 3) needles, cast on 61 sts, and work 1 row into back of cast-on sts.
*1st row:* *k1, p1, repeat from * to last stich, k1.
Repeat this row 10 times, decreasing once at end of last row.
*1st row:* Knit.

*2nd row:* k1, purl to last stitch, k1.
Repeat these 2 rows five times.
*13th row:* *k8, k2 tog, repeat from * to end of row.
*14th row and all alternate rows:* k1, purl to last stitch, k1.
*15th row:* *k7, k2 tog, repeat from* to end of row.
*17th row:* *k6, k2 tog, repeat from * to end of row.
Continue in stocking stitch, working 1st st less between decreases, until 6 sts remain.
Cast off.
The cap can be finished with a pompom, which can easily be made by winding the wool 80 times round four fingers. Tie through middle firmly and end off, leaving a length to sew pompom to cap. Cut the other end, and clip evenly all over to make a ball. Sew to top of cap.

## Coat

*Back*
Using 3.25 mm (10) (US 3) needles, cast on 41 sts, and work 1 row into the back of cast-on sts.
*1st row:* *k1, p1, repeat from * to last st, k1.
Repeat this row 8 times.
Work 16 rows in stocking st.
Cast off 3 sts at the beginning of each of the next 2 rows.
Dec once at each end of the needle in every alternative row twice.
Work 16 rows without shaping.
Cast off 5 sts at the beginning of each of the next 4 rows.
Cast off remaining sts.

*Right front*
Using 3.25 mm (10) (US 3) needles cast on 25 sts and work 1 row into back of the cast-on sts.
*1st row:* k1, p1, repeat from * to last st, k1.
Repeat row 8 times.
*10th row:* (k1, p1) three times, knit to end of row.
*11th row:* k1, purl to last 7 sts, (k1, p1) three times, k1.
Repeat 10th and 11th rows 7 times, then 10th row once.
Keeping the border of 7 sts in moss st at the centre edge, cast off 3 sts at the beginning of the next row.

Dec once at the end of the needle in the next and every alternate row, twice.

Work 11 rows without shaping.

Cast off 7 sts at the beginning of the needle in the next row.

Dec once at the neck edge in every alternate row until 10 sts remain, ending at the armhole edge.

Cast off 5 sts at the beginning of each of the next 2 rows.

### Left front

Work exactly as the right front, but working the border and shapings at the opposite end of the needle, and working buttonholes in the border in the 3rd and every following 10th row (5 buttonholes) as follows:

k1, p1, k1, wl fwd, k2 tog, p1, k1, work to end of row.

### Sleeves

Using 3.25 mm (10) (US 3) needles, cast on 19 sts and work 1 row into back of the cast-on sts.

*1st row:* *k1, p1, repeat from * to last st, k1. Repeat this row 8 times.

*10th row:* Increase once in the first stitch, k5, (inc once in next st, k5) twice, inc once in last st.

Working in stocking st, inc 1st at each end of the needle in every 4th row, until there are 29 sts on the needle.

Work 3 rows without shaping. (The sleeves may be made longer here if desired.)

Cast off 3 sts at the beginning of the needle in each of the next 2 rows, then dec once at each end of the needle in the next and every alternate row until 7 sts remain. Cast off.

Work another sleeve to match.

### Collar

Sew up the shoulder seams.

Knit up 41 sts around the neck to within 3 sts of the centre edge on each side.

*1st row:* *k1, p1, repeat from * to last stitch, k1.

Keeping the continuity of the moss st, increase once at each end of the needle in every 4th row three times. Work 2 rows. Cast off.

Press each part following instructions on page 6.

Sew sleeves into armholes, and then sew sleeve seams and side seams as one long seam.

# Legginettes

### Right leg

Using 3.25 mm (10) (US 3) needles, cast on 40 sts, and work 1 row into the back of the cast-on sts.

*1st row:* k2, *p1, k1, repeat from * to end of row. Repeat this row twice.

*4th row:* k1, *wl fwd, k2 tog, k1, repeat from * to end of row.

Repeat 1st row five times.

*10th row:* k30, turn.

*11th and alternate rows:* k1, purl to the last st, k1.

*12th row:* k20, turn.

*14th row:* k10, turn.

*15th row:* Repeat 11th row.

**Work 3 rows without shaping.

Inc once at the end of the needle in next and every following 4th row, until there are 43 sts on needle.

Work 8 rows without shaping

Dec once at each end of the needle in every 4th row three times, then dec once at each end of the needle in every alternate row, four times (29 sts).

Work 12 rows without shaping.

*Next row:* *k1, p1, repeat from *to last st, k1. Repeat this row three times.

Proceed as follows:

*1st row:* Cast off 14 sts, work in pattern to end of row.

*2nd row:* Cast off 3 sts, work in pattern to end of row.

Keeping the continuity of the moss st, dec once at each end of the needle in every row until 6 sts remain. Cast off.**

### Left leg

Work exactly the same as the right leg for the first 9 rows.

*10th and alternate rows:* Knit.

*11th row:* p30, turn.

*13th row:* p20, turn.

*15th row:* p10, turn.

*16th row:* Knit.

Work ** to ** as for right leg.

Press following directions on page 6, and sew up side, centre and leg seams.

# Shoes

Using 2.75 mm (12) (US 1) needles, cast on 24 sts and work 1 row into the back of the cast-on sts.

*1st row:* k1, inc once in next st, k8, inc once in next st, k2, inc once in next st, k8, inc once in next st, k1.

*2nd and alternate rows:* Knit.

*3rd row:* k1, inc, k10, inc, k2, inc, k10, inc, k1.

*5th row:* k14, inc, k2, inc, k14.

*7th row:* k15, inc, k2, inc, k15.

Work 6 rows in garter st without shaping.

*1st row:* k23, turn.

*2nd row:* k10, turn.

*3rd row:* k9, k2 tog, turn.

Repeat 3rd row until 10 sts remain each side.

*Next row:* Knit to end of row.

*Next row:* k1, *wl fwd, k2 tog, k1, repeat from * to last 2 sts, wl fwd, k2 tog.

Cast off.

Work another shoe in the same manner.

Sew up sole and back seam.

# Noel *illustrated on page 40*

A delightful set of clothes to suit a 30 cm (12") doll of the 1940s era which is equally at home on any doll of this size. The set consists of a pair of combinations, a jumper, pants, beret and, if you wish, shoettes.

## Materials

50g (2 oz) Patons 3-ply baby wool in desired colour
25g (1 oz) Patons 3-ply baby wool in white for the combinations
Pair 3 mm (11) (US 3) knitting needles
Pair 2.75 mm (12) (US 2) knitting needles
Crochet hook 2 mm (14) (US A)
Small amount silk crochet cotton for the neck of the combinations (optional)
3 small buttons

## Measurements

| | |
|---|---|
| *Jumper:* From shoulder to bottom | 12 cm (5") |
| Width around at underarm | 24 cm (9½") |
| Length of sleeve to underarm | 7 cm (2¾") |
| *Pants:* Length at front | 11 cm (4½") |
| *Combinations:* Length from front neck to crutch | 13 cm (5¼") |
| Length from shoulder to hip | 13 cm (5¼") |
| *Beret:* Circumference unstretched | 20 cm (8") |

## Tension

8 sts in width, 11 rows in depth over 2.5 cm (1") of smooth fabric.

See page 10 for abbreviations.

# Combinations

*Front*
With 3 mm (11) (US 3) needles cast on 10 sts.
Knit 1 row. Purl 1 row.
Continue in stocking st, casting on 2 sts at the beginning of every row until you have 34 sts on the needle.
Work 20 rows straight in stocking st, then 4 rows in k1, p1 rib, and then work 4 more rows in stocking st.
To shape the armholes:
Cast off 2 sts at the beginning of every row until you have 22 sts on the needle.
Work 3 rows in stocking st.
*Next row:* k 8, turn, and purl to end.
Continue in stocking st on these 8 sts, but k2 tog at neck edge in the following next 2 knit rows (6 sts).

Work 3 rows on these 6 sts (for the shoulder) and cast off. (Should you wish to make the combinations a little longer, just increase the number of rows of sts here, remembering to do the same on the other parts of the garment.)
Rejoin wool to unworked sts, cast off 6 sts, and knit to end.
Purl one row.
K2 tog at the beginning of the following 2 knit rows (6 sts).
Work 3 rows on these 6 sts and cast off.

*Back*
Work the same as the front until 13 rows have been worked in stocking st on the 34 sts, then divide the sts for centre back opening as follows:
*Left half back:*
*1st row:* p15, k4 for border, turn (leaving 15 sts unworked).
*2nd row:* Knit 19.
Repeat the last 2 rows twice more, then the 1st row again.
Work 4 rows in k1, p1 rib, making sure you keep the 4 st border in garter st.
*1st buttonhole row:* k2, cast off 2 sts, knit to end.
*2nd buttonhole row:* p15, cast on 2 sts, k2.
Work 4 rows in stocking st with k4 border.
**To shape the armhole:
Cast off 2 sts (at armhole end) of the next row and following 2 alternate rows (13 sts).
Purl 1 row.
Work buttonhole as before in the next two rows.
To shape neck:
Cast off 4 sts, knit to end (9 sts).
K2 tog at the neck edge of next 3 rows.
Work 1 row and cast off.**

*Right half back:*
Rejoin wool to the 15 sts left unworked, pick up and knit 4 sts at back of garter st border, purl to end of row.
Keeping the 4 st border in garter st, work 6 rows in stocking st, and then 4 rows in k1, p1 rib.
Work 4 rows in stocking st, and then continue from ** to ** of left half back, omitting buttonholes.

*To make up*
Press following instructions on page 6. Join shoulder seams and crutch seam. Sew two buttons to the garter st border to correspond with the buttonholes.

*To finish armholes and neck*

Using either the same wool or crochet silk, work a small picot edge around armholes and neck as follows (American readers please refer to page 11 for translation of crochet terms):

Using 2 mm (14) (US A) crochet hook, work 1 dc into first st around neck, in next st work 1 dc, 3 chain, and slip st into 1st loop of chain. Repeat around neck edge, but not down garter st border. Work the armholes in the same manner.

# Pants

*Front*

With 3 mm (11) (US 3) needles, cast on 10 sts and knit 1 row, purl 1 row.

Continue in stocking st, casting on 2 sts at the beginning of every row 12 times, then 3 sts at the beginning of the next 2 rows (40 sts).

Work 10 rows in stocking st.

Dec 1 st at each end of the next row and following 8th row (36 sts).

Work 5 rows in stocking st.

Work 4 rows in k1, p1, rib.

*Slot row:* k1, *m1, k2 tog, repeat from * until 1 st remains, p1.

Rib 3 rows. Cast off.

*Back*

Work the same as the front.

*Leg bands*

First join the side seams. Using 2.75 mm (12) (US 2) needles, pick up 34 sts all around one leg edge and work 5 rows loosely in k1, p1 rib. Cast off loosely in rib.

Work other leg band to match.

*To make up*

Press, then join the leg seam. Thread ribbon, elastic or a crochet chain through the slots at the waist.

# Jumper

*Front:*

Using 3 mm (11) (US 3) needles, cast on 39 sts; work 6 rows in k1, p1 rib and then 2 rows in stocking st, beginning with a knit row.

*1st row* (of pattern): *p1, then knit into the front, back and front again of the next st. Slip the 3rd st from the point of the right-hand needle over the two end sts. Repeat from * until 1 st remains, p1. (This may sound complicated but is very easy to master and do.)

*2nd row:* *k1, p2 tog, repeat from * until 1 st remains, k1.

*3rd row:* Knit.

*4th row:* Purl.

Work the 4 pattern rows once, then 1st and 2nd rows again.

Work 10 rows in stocking st.

To shape armholes:

Cast off 2 sts at the beginning of the next 2 rows, then dec at each end of following 4 alternate rows (27 sts).

Work 3 rows in stocking st, ending with a purl row.

*Next row:* k9, cast off 9, k9.

*Continuing on these last 9 sts, k2 tog at neck edge in every alternate row until 6 sts remain.

Work 2 rows. Cast off.*

Rejoin wool, and repeat from * to * for the other side of front neck.

*Back*

Work as for front until the 4th armhole decrease row has been worked (27 sts).

Work 12 rows in stocking st. Cast off.

Sew up right shoulder seam.

*Neck edging*

With right side of work facing and starting at the left shoulder, with 3 mm (11) (US 3) needles, pick up and knit 48 sts around neck. Work 3 rows loosely in k1, p1 rib. Cast off loosely in rib, to enable jumper to stretch over doll's head.

*Sleeves*

With 3 mm (11) (US 3) needles, cast on 21 sts and work 4 rows in k1, p1 rib.

Continue in stocking st, inc 1 st at each end of the 3rd, and then every 4th row, until the 6th inc row has been worked (33 sts).

Work 3 rows in stocking st.

To shape sleeve:

Dec 1 st at beginning of next 6 rows, and then the following alternate row.

Cast off the remaining 25 sts.

Work another sleeve in the same way.

*To make up*

Press following instructions on page 6. Set the sleeves into the armholes, first placing the front shoulder on the left, over the back, for about 2 cm (¾").

Join the sleeve and side seams. Work a button loop on the front shoulder, and stitch a small button onto the back shoulder to fasten.

# Beret

With 3 mm (11) (US 3) needles, cast on 60 sts.

Work 6 rows in k1, p1 rib.

*1st row* (right side of work): *k5, inc in next st, repeat from * to end of row.

*2nd row:* Purl.

*3rd row:* *k6, inc, repeat from * to end.

*4th row:* Purl.

GEOFFREY

**GEOFFREY** The smallest doll in this book, this 15 cm (6") hard plastic, straight-legged Suzy doll is an example of the many small dolls of this type manufactured in England and Australia in the 1950s and 1960s. Beside him stands a tiny fur bear made in Poland. Pattern on page 25.

TREVOR

**TREVOR** Typical of the 18–19 cm (7"–7½") hard plastic dolls that were sold in their thousands in the 1950s and 1960s, this small doll by Pedigree (England) with his star-shaped hands is standing beside a ⅛th scale rocking chair made by Jim Fainges as a Sydney Doll Convention gift several years ago. Pattern on page 57.

**MICHAEL**

**MICHAEL** Surprised by the unusual 'Cat' jack-in-the-box, made in Germany before 1940, the bisque headed doll wearing his smart three-piece suit and matching shoes is a 352 2½ Armand Marseille doll, 'Baby Love', which has the celluloid arms and legs and cloth body denoting it was assembled in Australia during the late 1930s. Pattern on page 35.

**NOEL**

**NOEL** This small 30 cm (12") composition doll, nursing a small fur dog of early vintage with soulful eyes, could have been made in the USA, England or Australia. In fact he is the composition baby doll made by Trio in Stawell, Victoria in the 1940s–1950s. This firm made over 1000 dolls a week during the years they operated in a country town west of Melbourne. Pattern on page 37.

Continue increasing as per the 3rd and 4th rows, with 1 st more between the increases, 3 times (100 sts) finishing with a purl row.

Work in pattern as follows:

*1st row:* *p1, knit into the front, back and front again of next st, slip the 3rd st over the two end sts, repeat from * until 2 sts remain, p1, k1.

*2nd row:* k2, *p2 tog, k1, repeat from * to end.

*3rd row:* Knit

*4th row:* Purl.

Repeat the last 4 rows once.

*1st dec row:* *k8, k2 tog, repeat from * to end of row.

*2nd and all alternate rows:* Purl

*3rd row:* *k7, k2 tog, repeat from * to end of row.

Continue in this way, working 1 st less between k2 tog in every 2nd row, until you have worked *k2 tog, repeat * all along row.

Cut the wool leaving enough to thread a needle, and thread through the remaining sts. Draw up all stitches tightly together and secure well. Sew up seam.

Press beret. It can either be left plain, or decorated with a small pompom, stitched in place on centre top of beret.

# Shoettes

Using 2.75 mm (12) (US 2) needles, cast on 22 sts.
Work 4 rows in k1, p1 rib, and then 6 rows in stocking st, beginning with a knit row.

*Instep*
k14, turn, p6, turn, leaving 8 sts unworked at each side.
Work 12 rows in garter st on the centre 6 sts. Break off wool.
With right side of work facing, rejoin wool to bottom of instep, pick up and knit 6 sts from the side of the instep, k6 sts across top of instep, pick up and k6 sts down other side of instep, and then work the 8 sts from the other side of the work (34 sts)
Work 7 rows in garter st. Cast off.
Work another shoette the same.
Thread hat elastic through ribbing to hold shoette on doll's foot.

# *Peter*  *illustrated on page 49*

A 'Buster' suit suitable for a 41 cm (16") doll. Coats Patons have kindly given permission to reproduce this 1950s–1960s pattern from their Knitting Book C.5. The pattern has been slightly adapted to suit today's idiom and materials. This 4-piece suit, including blazer, shirt, pants and cap, is ideally suited to the many hard plastic dolls that were manufactured in the 1950s and 1960s, but like all the others in this book it is a classic boy's pattern and can be used on dolls of any age and type.

## Materials:

100 g (4 oz) Patonyle 4-ply in main colour (MC) for pants, blazer and cap
50 g (2 oz) Patonyle 4-ply in contrast colour (C) (white)—for pants and shirt
Pair 3.25 mm (10) (US 3) knitting needles
Crochet hook, 2.75 mm (12) (US C)
9 buttons to match MC (3 for blazer, 6 on shirt to attach pants)
3 small pearl buttons for shirt

## Measurements

| | |
|---|---|
| *Shirt* From top of shoulder | 11 cm (4½") |
| Width around at underarm (fastened) | 30 cm (12") |
| Length of sleeve seam | 3.5 cm (1½") |
| *Pants:* Front seam | 11 cm (4½") |
| Width around at waist | 32 cm (13") |
| *Blazer:* Length from top of shoulder | 14 cm (5½") |
| Width around at underarm (fastened) | 31 cm (12¼") |
| Length of sleeve seam | 6.5 cm (2½") |
| *Cap* circumference (unstretched) | 28 cm (11") |

## Tension

8 sts in width, 10 rows in depth over 2.5 cm (1") over smooth fabric.

See page 10 for abbreviations.

## Pants

*Left leg*
Using 3.25 mm (10) (US 3) needles and MC, cast on 59 sts.
*1st row:* (MC) k1, purl to last st, k1. Join in C, but do not break off MC, twisting the yarns under and over each other at side of work.
*2nd row:* p1 (C), *keeping C wool to front of work, sl 1 (MC) purlwise, p1 (C). Repeat from * to end of row.
*3rd row;* p1 (C), *pass C wool to back of work, sl 1 (MC) knitwise. Bring C wool to front and p1 (C). Repeat from * to end of row.

*4th row:* (MC) k1, purl to last st, k1.
These 4 rows complete one pattern for pants.
Work 1 more complete pattern.
Keeping continuity of pattern, cast off 2 sts at beginning of next 3 rows (53 sts).
Continue in pattern until 13 complete patterns have been worked, ending with a 4th pattern row. Break off C.
To shape back:
*1st row:* (MC) k1, purl to last 10 sts, turn. Break off MC, join in C.
*2nd row:* (C) Work 2nd row pattern to end of row.
*3rd row:* Work 3rd row pattern to last 20 sts, turn, break off C, join in MC.
*4th row:* (MC) Purl to last st, k1.
*5th row:* k1, purl to last 30 sts, turn, break off MC, join in C.
*6th row:* Work 2nd row pattern to end of row.
*7th row:* Work 3rd row pattern to last 40 sts, turn, break off C, join in MC.
*8th row:* Purl to last st, k1.
***9th row:* k3, *k2 tog, k3, repeat from * to end of row (43 sts).
Knit 2 rows.
*12th row* (buttonholes): k7, (wl fwd, k2 tog, k12) twice, wl fwd, k2 tog, k6.
Knit 2 rows. cast off loosely**.

*Right leg*
With MC cast on 59 sts, and work 2 complete patterns, then 1st row of next pattern. Keeping continuity of pattern, cast off 2 sts at beginning of next 3 rows (53 sts).
Continue in pattern until the 3rd row of 13 patterns has been worked from the beginning.
To shape back:
*1st row:* (MC) k1, purl to last 10 sts, turn.
*2nd row:* (MC) purl to last st, k1.
*3rd row:* Work 2nd row pattern to last 20 sts, turn.
*4th row:* Work 3rd row pattern to end of row.
*5th row:* (MC) k1, purl to last 30 sts, turn.
*6th row:* (MC) purl to last st, k1.
*7th row:* Work 2nd row pattern to last 40 sts, turn.

*8th row:* Work 3rd row pattern to end of row.

Break off both wools. Slip sts from one needle onto the other needle.

With right side of work facing, join in MC, and repeat from ** to ** as given for left leg.

# Shirt

This is worked in one piece (up the back and down the front, without seams at shoulders).

Beginning at lower edge of back, with C wool and 3.25 mm (10) (US 3) needles, cast on 44 sts and work 4 rows in k1, p1 rib.

Work 16 rows in stocking st. (If you want a longer shirt, work more rows of stocking st, remembering to do the same number of extra rows when working the two fronts.)

Cast on 10 sts at the beginning of next 2 rows, for the sleeves (64 sts), keeping 2 sts at each end of the needle in garter st.

Work 21 rows of stocking st on these 64 sts, ending with a knit row.

*Next row:* k2, p22, cast off 16 sts for neck, p22, k2.

Working on last 24 sts, and keeping 2 sts in garter st at cuff edge as before, work 12 rows in stocking st, ending at neck edge.

Cast on 10 sts for front of neck.

*Next row:* k2, purl to last 2 sts, k2.

Keeping 2 sts in garter st at each end of work, continue in stocking st for 12 rows, ending at cuff edge.

*Next row:* Cast off 10 sts, thus finishing sleeve. Knit to end of row (24 sts).

Keeping 2 sts in garter st at front edge, continue in stocking st until side edge measures same as back to ribbing.

Work 4 rows in k1, p1 rib. Cast off loosely in rib.

With right side of work facing, join in wool to remaining 24 sts, and continue, corresponding to other side, until sts are cast on at front of neck.

*Next row* (1st buttonhole): k2, wl fwd, k2 tog, knit to end of row.

Work 2 more buttonholes, 12 rows apart, and continue, corresponding to other side.

With wrong side of work facing, and using C wool, pick up and knit 44 sts around neck for collar (starting behind the 2 garter st front border, and ending before it).

Knit 10 rows in garter st, and cast off loosely.

*To make up suit*

Press following instructions on page 6. Sew up leg, front and back seams of pants. Sew up side seams of shirt. Sew buttons to shirt to correspond to buttonholes, and sew 6 contrasting buttons 2.5 cm (1") above lower edge of shirt to correspond with buttonholes on pants. Button pants to shirt.

# Blazer

*Back*

With MC and 3.25 mm (10) (US 3) needles, cast on 48 sts. Work 26 rows in stocking st.

To shape armholes:

Cast off 2 sts at beginning of next 2 rows, then dec 1 st at each end of needle in next and following alternate row (40 sts).

Continue in stocking st until 47 rows have been worked from beginning, ending with a knit row.

*Next row:* k1, p11, cast off 16 sts, p11, k1.

Working on last 12 sts, knit 1 row, purl 1 row, cast off.

With right side of work facing, join wool to remaining 12 sts, and knit 1 row, purl 1 row.

Cast off.

*Left front*

With MC cast on 21 sts.

*1st row:* Knit to last 2 sts, inc 1 st in next st, k1 (front edge).

*2nd row:* Inc 1 st in 1st st, purl to last st, k1.

Repeat these 2 rows once (25 sts).

Knit 1 row, purl 1 row.

*7th row* (1st buttonhole): Knit to last 2 sts, wl fwd, k2 tog.

Working 2nd buttonhole on following 10th row, and 3rd buttonhole in 10th row from 2nd buttonhole, continue in stocking st until 26 rows have been worked from beginning, ending at side edge.

To shape armhole:

Cast off 2 sts at armhole edge, then dec 1 st in alternate rows twice, ending at front edge.

To shape neck:

Dec 1 st at neck edge on next and every alternate row until 12 sts remain.

Continue in stocking st until 50 rows have been worked from the bottom edge. Cast off.

*Right front*

With MC cast on 21 sts.

*1st row* (front edge): Inc 1 st in 1st st, knit to end of row.

*2nd row:* k1, purl to last 2 sts, inc 1 st in next st, k1.

Repeat these 2 rows once (25 sts).

Omitting buttonholes, continue to correspond to left front, being careful to have all shapings on opposite side of work.

*Sleeves*

With MC cast on 34 sts, and work 20 rows in stocking st, ending with purl row.

To shape top:

*Cast off 2 sts at beginning of next 2 rows, then 1 st at beginning of the following 2 rows*.

Repeat from * to * until 10 sts remain. Cast off.

Work another sleeve in the same manner.

*Pockets* (make 2)

With MC cast on 11 sts, and work 8 rows in stocking st. Continue in stocking st, dec 1 st at each end of needle twice. Cast off.

*To make up*

Press following instructions on page 6. Sew up all seams. Sew in sleeves. With C crochet 2 rows double crochet (US sc) around cuffs, cast-on edge of each pocket and entire edge of blazer. Sew pockets in position and sew on buttons to correspond with buttonholes.

# Cap

With MC and 3.25 mm (10) (US 3) needles, cast on 84 sts, and work 4 rows in k1, p1 rib.

Work 12 rows in stocking st, ending with a purl row.
To shape top:
*1st row:* *k12, k2 tog, repeat from * to end of row.
*2nd and alternate rows:* k1, purl to last st, k1.
*3rd row:* *k11, k2 tog, repeat from * to end of row.
*5th row:* *k10, k2 tog, repeat from * to end of row.
Continue decreasing in this manner, that is, having 1 st less between k2 tog stitches, in every alternate row, until 24 sts remain, ending with purl row.
*Next row:* (k2 tog) 12 times. Break off wool. Thread end through remaining sts. Draw up and fasten securely. Sew up back seam.
If you wish make a small pompom in MC and sew to top of cap.

# Sammy *illustrated on page 50*

Courtesy of Coats Patons, this pattern has been adapted to suit today's materials. The outfit, consisting of beret, jumper, pants and shoe/sock combination, can be made in two sizes simply by using different ply wools and different sized needles.

## LARGER DOLL

### Materials

1 ball Patons 4-ply Patonyle in MC
1 ball Patons 4-ply Patonyle in C
Pair 3.25 mm (10) (US 3) needles
Pair 2.75 mm (12) (US 2) needles
Medium-sized crochet hook
Ribbon or elastic
2 buttons

### Measurements

| | |
|---|---|
| *Jumper* From top of shoulder | 14 cm (5½") |
| Width around at underarm | 26 cm (10") |
| *Pants* Length at centre front | 12 cm (4¾") |
| *Beret* Circumference | 24 cm (9") |
| *Shoes* Length | 5 cm (2") |

### Tension

8 sts in width, 9½ rows in depth = 2.5 cm (1") over smooth fabric.

## SMALLER DOLL

### Materials

1 ball Patons 3-ply Baby Wool in MC
1 ball Patons 3-ply Baby Wool in C
Pair 2.75 mm (12) (US 2) needles
Pair 2 mm (14) (US 0) needles
2 mm (14) (US B) crochet hook
Ribbon or elastic
2 buttons

### Measurements

| | |
|---|---|
| *Jumper* From top of shoulder | 10.5 cm (4¼") |
| Width around at underarm | 20 cm (8") |
| *Pants* Length at centre front | 9.5 cm (3¼") |
| *Beret* Circumference | 16 cm (6½") |
| *Shoe* Length | 3 cm (1¼") |

### Tension

10 sts in width, 12 rows in depth = 2.5 cm (1") over smooth fabric.

See page 10 for abbreviations.

Instructions for smaller size are given in square brackets [].

## Jumper (back and front alike)

With 2.75 mm (12) (US 2) [2 mm (14) (US 0)] needles and MC, cast on 37 sts, and work 8 rows in k1, p1 rib.
Change to 3.25 mm (10) (US 3) [2.75 mm (12) (US 2)] needles and C and work 2 rows k1, p1 rib. Join in MC again, and work 2 rows in stocking stitch.
These 4 rows constitute the pattern.
Repeat the last 4 rows 5 times, then shape armholes by decreasing at each end of next 4 alternate rows.
Work straight for 3 patterns, and then work the first 7 sts, leaving the rest on a spare needle.
On these 7 stitches work 1 pattern and cast off. Return to spare needle and cast off all sts but the last 7; work on these 7 sts to correspond with other shoulder and cast off.

*Sleeves*
With 2.75 mm (12) (US 2) [(2 mm (14) (US 0)] needles and MC cast on 21 sts.
Work 6 rows in k1, p1 rib, then change to 3.25 mm (10) (US 3) [2.75 mm (12) (US 2)] needles and, working in pattern, increase at each end of every 4th row until there are 35 sts.
Then continue in pattern until 8 patterns have been worked from the beginning.
To shape top, decrease at each end of next and every alternate row, until 27 sts remain.
Cast off.

*To make up*
Press all pieces with a warm iron on the wrong side. Join side seams and insert sleeves. Work a row of double crochet (US sc) around neck edge, making loops for buttonholes at shoulder. Sew on buttons to match loops.

# Pants (back and front alike)

With 3.25 mm (10) (US 3) [2.75 mm (12) (US 2)] needles and MC, cast on 12 sts and knit 1 row.
Working in stocking stitch, cast on 3 sts at beginning of every row until there are 42 sts.
Work 8 rows straight, then decrease at each end of next and following 8th row.
Work straight for 12 rows, then work 4 rows k1, p1 rib.
Make a row of holes for elastic:
Rib 2, (m1, rib 2 tog, rib 1) 12 times.
Work 3 more rows in rib, then cast off in rib.
Make another piece the same.
Join crutch seam, and then with 2.75 mm (12) (US 2) [2 mm (14) (US 0)] needles and front of work facing you, pick up and knit 43 sts around each leg.
Work 3 rows in k1, p1 rib. Cast off in rib.
To make up, press lightly with a warm iron on the wrong side and then join both side seams.

# Beret

With 2.75 mm (12) (US 2) [2 mm (14) (US 0)] needles and MC, cast on 55 sts, and work 4 rows k1, p1 rib.
Start increasing for head:
Change to 3.25 mm (10) (US 3) [2.75 mm (12) (US 2)] needles.
*1st row:* *k4, knit twice into next st, repeat from * to end.
*2nd row and next three alternate rows:* Purl.
*3rd row:* *k5, inc in next st, repeat from * to end.
*5th row:* *k6, inc in next st, repeat from * to end.
*7th row:* *k7, inc in next st, repeat from * to end.
Work 6 rows of striped pattern for jumper, starting with C, then change to MC and stocking st.

*1st row:* *k7, k2 tog, repeat from * to end.
*2nd row and all alternate rows:* Purl.
*3rd row:* *k6, k2 tog, repeat from * to end.
*5th row:* *k5, k2 tog, repeat from * to end.
*7th row:* *k4, k2 tog, repeat from * to end.
Continue decreasing in this way until you have worked k2 tog all along row, then break off wool, leaving a long end. Thread wool through needle and thread through remaining sts, draw up wool and fasten off. Sew up seam.

# Shoes/socks

With 2.75 mm (12) (US 2) [2 mm (14) (US 0)] needles and MC, cast on 22 sts.
Work 4 rows in k1, p1 rib.
Work 6 rows in striped pattern as for jumper, starting with C.
With MC, make a row of holes for ribbon or elastic: k1, (wl fwd, k2 tog, k1) seven times.
*Next row:* Purl.
Slip the first 8 sts onto a safety pin. Work across the next 6 sts in pattern, slip the last 8 sts onto a safety pin.
Continue on centre 6 sts in striped pattern until 6 C stripes have been worked. Break off wool.
With right side facing and using MC, work the first 8 sts from safety pin, pick up and knit 6 sts up side of centre piece just worked, work the 6 sts from top of centre piece, pick up 6 more sts down other side of centre piece, and then work 8 sts from second safety pin. Knit 6 rows in garter st.
*1st row:* k13, k2 tog, k4, k2 tog, k13.
*2nd row:* k2 tog at each end of needle (for heel).
*3rd row:* k11, k2 tog, k4, k2 tog, k11.
*4th row:* k2 tog at each end of needle. Cast off.
Make another shoe/sock to match. Sew up back seam and sole of foot.

# Stephen *illustrated on page 51*

A delightful outfit including hat, sleeveless shirt, jacket, pants and shoes, to fit a 40–46 cm (16"–18") composition or celluloid doll. Adapted from the 1930s book *Knitted Sets for Dolls*, this classic suit for a boy doll will look equally elegant on a hard plastic or modern vinyl doll. Using finer ply wool and smaller needles, this outfit can also be made to fit a smaller doll.

## Materials
50 g (2 oz) Bendigo 3-ply fingering wool in MC (hat, jacket, pants and shoes)
25 g (1 oz) Bendigo 3-ply fingering wool in C (sleeveless shirt)
Pair 3.25 mm (10) (US 3) knitting needles
Medium-sized crochet hook
4 small buttons for shirt
2 matching coloured buttons for shoes
5 larger buttons (4 to button on pants and 1 for jacket)
3 snap fasteners (press-studs)

## Measurements
| | | |
|---|---|---|
| *Jacket* From top of shoulder to hem | 16.5 cm (6½") | |
| Width around at underarm (open) | 28 cm (11") | |
| Length of sleeve seam | 12 cm (4¾") or length desired | |
| *Pants* Length of front seam | 13 cm (5¼") | |
| Length of inside leg seam | 7.5 cm (3") | |
| *Shirt* From top of shoulder to hem | 15 cm (6") | |
| Width around at underarm (unstretched) | 28 cm (11") (this pattern stretches easily) | |
| *Hat* Circumference (unstretched) | 30.5 cm (12") | |
| *Shoes* Sole | 6 cm (2¼") | |

## Tension
8 sts in width, 9 rows in depth over 2.5 cm (1") of smooth fabric.

See page 10 for abbreviations.

## Pants

*With 3.25 mm (10) (US 3) needles, cast on 46 sts (for one leg).
Work 3 rows in garter st.
*4th row:* k8, cast off 3 sts, knit to last 11 sts, cast off 3 sts, knit to end.
*5th row:* k8, cast on 3 sts, knit to last 11 sts, cast on 3 sts, k8.

*6th row:* Knit (work into back of cast-on sts of previous row).
*7th and 8th rows:* Knit*.
Work 4 rows in stocking st.
Pants back shaping:
*1st row:* k8, turn, purl back.
*3rd row:* k16, turn, purl back.
*5th row:* k24, turn, purl back.
Continue in this way until all 46 sts on the needle have been worked.
*Next row:* Purl.
Continue in stocking st, increasing 1 st at the beginning of next and every 4th row, until 52 sts are on needle.
**Work 9 rows in stocking st.
Dec 1 st at both ends of the needle on every row until 40 sts remain.
Work 10 rows in k1, p1 rib. Cast off loosely in rib.**.
Work second leg as follows:
Work in rib from * to * of first leg.
Work in stocking st for 5 rows, ending with a knit row.
*1st row* (shaping): p8, turn and knit back.
*3rd row:* p16, turn and knit back.
*5th row:* p24, turn and knit back.
Continue in this way until all 46 sts have been worked.
*Next row:* Knit.
Continue in stocking st, inc 1 st at end of next and every 4th row, until 52 sts are on needle.
Finish leg by working from ** to ** of first leg.

*To make up*
Press following instructions on page 6. Sew up front, back and leg seams.
If a more modern look is required, turn under rib at bottom of leg.

## Jacket

With 3.25 mm (10) (US 3) needles and MC, cast on 80 sts and knit 9 rows in garter st.
*1st row:* knit.
*2nd row:* k6, purl to last 6 sts, k6.
Repeat last 2 rows, 14 times.

Armholes:
Work 18 sts, cast off 6 sts, work 32 sts (including st actually on right needle), cast off 6 sts, work to end.
On the last 18 sts work 18 rows in stocking st.

*Neck*
** Starting at front (border) edge, cast off 8 sts.
Work on the remaining 10 sts for 7 rows. Cast off.**
Rejoin wool to 32 sts, and starting with a purl row, work in st st for 26 rows.
Rejoin wool to final 18 sts, and starting with a purl row, work 19 rows.
Work neck shaping ** to ** as for other side.

*Sleeves*
Cast on 36 sts and work in garter st for 9 rows.
Change to stocking st and work 38 rows or length desired.
Shape top:
Cast off 3 sts at beginning of every row until 12 sts remain.
Cast off.

*Collar*
Cast on 12 sts and work 8 rows in garter st.
*1st row:* p8, k4.
*2nd row:* Knit.
Repeat these two rows, 30 times.
Work 7 rows in garter st. Cast off.

*To make up*
Sew shoulder seams. Insert sleeves into armholes and sew up sleeve and side seams. With right sides of work facing, attach collar, working from 2 sts inside front edge to 2 sts inside other front edge, easing to fit neck edge. Make a buttonhole loop near top edge, and close jacket with button. If doll has short arms, turn back cuffs.

# Cap

Using 3.25 mm (10) (US 3) needles and main colour, cast on 80 sts.
Work 16 rows in garter st.
Beginning with a purl row, work 3 rows in stocking st.
*Next row:* *k8, k2 tog, repeat from * to end (70 sts).
Work 13 rows in stocking st.
*1st row:* *k7, k2 tog, repeat from * to end.
*2nd and alternate rows:* Purl.
*3rd row:* *k6, k2 tog, repeat from * to end.
*5th row:* *k5, k2 tog, repeat from * to end.
Continue in this way until there is only 1 st between each k2 tog.
Break off wool, leaving a long enough end to thread wool into a darning needle, draw up remaining sts and fasten off securely. Sew up cap and turn back garter st border.

# Shoes

Using 3.25 mm (10) (US 3) needles and main colour, cast on 21 sts.
Knit 1 row.
*1st row:* k1, inc in next st, k7, inc in next st, k1, inc in next st, k7, inc in next st, k1.
*2nd and alternate rows:* Knit.
*3rd row:* k1, inc in next st, k9, inc in next st, k1, inc in next st, k9, inc in next st, k1.
*5th row:* k1, inc in next st, k11, inc in next st, k1, inc in next st, k11, inc in next st, k1.
*7th row:* k1, inc in next st, k13, inc in next st, k1, inc in next st, k13, inc in next st, k1.
Knit 5 rows.
*Next row:* k22, k2 tog, turn.
*Next row:* *sl 1, k8, k2 tog*.
Repeat from * to * until 28 sts remain altogether.
Knit right across needle. Cast off.
Sew up back seam and sole of foot.

---

*Opposite:* **PETER**  A typical doll of his size, 38–40 cm (15"–16"), Peter is examining a tinplate fire-engine made in Japan in the 1950s–1960s. This type of doll was manufactured in hard plastic in both Australia and England, and it is only by checking the marking on the back that you can identify the doll; in this case the marking is Patsy. Pattern on page 42.

*Page 50:* **SAMMY**  These two hard plastic dolls, typical of the dolls manufactured in Australia and England in the 1950s–1960s, are wearing the same outfit, which has been made in two different ply wools with different needles. The small 26 cm (10") doll with bent baby legs can have several different markings, but this one carries the Cherub trademark. The larger doll showing his small friend a metal motorbike is a 38–40 cm (15"–16") Patsy baby doll. Both dolls were made in Australia. Pattern on page 45.

*Page 51:* **STEPHEN**  A lovely example of a 48 cm (19") Polish celluloid doll, showing what you can do with the same outfit with very small alterations. On the right the doll is wearing the shirt open-neck style, with the bottom cuffs of the pants turned up underneath— so typical of a football costume, even today. (Why not knit this outfit in your team's colours?) The other outfit, with the same doll holding a puppet monkey with celluloid head (reminiscent of the 1930s to go with the date of the original pattern), portrays a much earlier style of clothing, and strikingly shows how a doll can alter its appearance just by a change of clothing. Pattern on page 47.

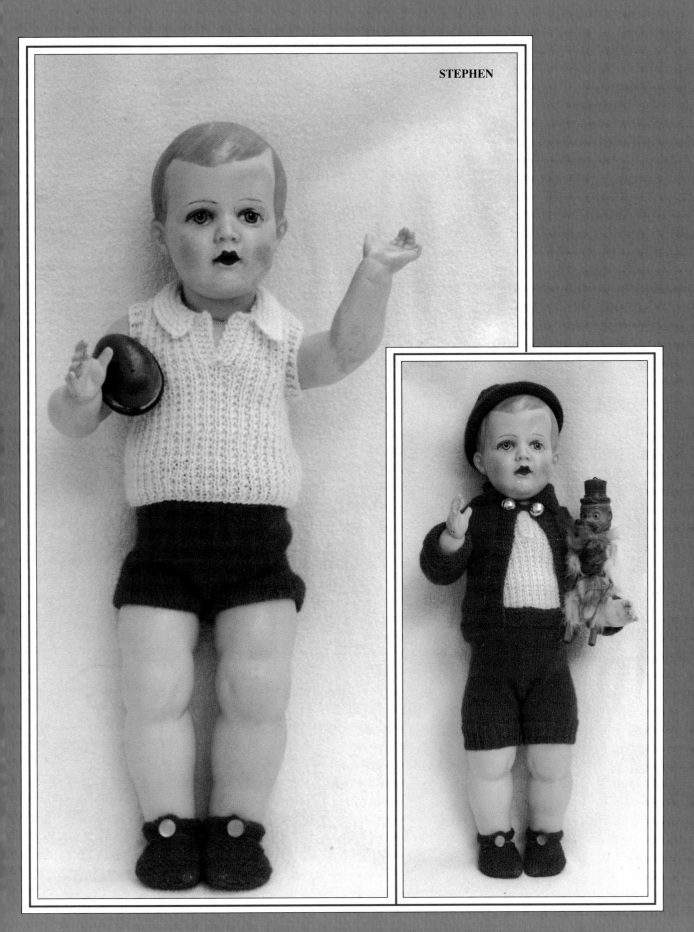

STEPHEN

*Strap*

Cast on 15 sts, pick up and knit 3 sts each side of back seam, cast on 15 sts (36 sts).

Knit 1 row through back of sts.

*Next row:* k2, wl fwd, k2 tog, knit to end.

*Next row:* Knit. Cast off.

Work another shoe the same way, working buttonhole in strap thus:

Knit to last 3 sts, wl fwd, k2 tog, k1.

Sew a small button on strap so that shoe can button up around ankle.

# Shirt

A very versatile garment. Buttoned up it can be worn as a dress shirt under a jacket, or unbuttoned can be a sports shirt. Can be finished on either side as it is a fully reversible pattern.

*Back*

With 3.25 mm (10) (US 3) needles and contrast wool, cast on 46 sts.

Work 4 rows in k1, p1 rib.

*1st row:* Knit.

*2nd row:* *k1, p1, repeat from * to end.

These two rows form the pattern. Repeat pattern 5 times.

Decrease 1 st at both ends of next row and following 4th row.

Continue in pattern for 16 rows.

Armhole:

Cast off 6 sts at the beginning of next 2 rows.

Continue in pattern for 28 rows.

Cast off 8 sts at beginning of next 2 rows. Leave the remaining 18 sts on a spare needle.

*Front*

Work as back to armholes.

Shape armholes and front opening:

Cast off 6 sts, k15, cast on 3 sts.

*Next row:* k3, work in pattern to end.

*Next row:* Knit.

Work the last two rows, 7 times (14 rows).

Neck edge:

**Cast off 6 sts, and work to end of row.

Dec 1 st at neck edge in every alternate row until 8 sts remain.

Work 2 rows. Cast off.**

Join in wool at centre front and cast on 3 sts, knit to end.

*Next row:* Cast off 6 sts, work in pattern to last 3 sts, k3.

Work 14 rows in pattern.

Neck edge:

Work in pattern from ** to ** on other side of front.

*To make up*

Join shoulder seams. Pick up 40 sts around armhole and work in k1, p1 rib for 4 rows. Cast off loosely in rib. Repeat for other armhole.

*Collar*

With right side facing, and starting 2 sts in from front edge, pick up and knit 16 sts up side of neck to back, knit 18 sts from spare needle at back, pick up and knit 16 sts down other front, ending 2 sts in from front edge.

*1st row:* Knit.

*2nd row:* k1, inc, knit to 2nd last st, inc, k1.

Repeat last 2 rows, 3 times.

Knit 4 rows. Cast off loosely.

*To make up*

Sew up side seams. Sew two snap fasteners (press-studs) down front, and on top side sew two small buttons if you wish to have the shirt closed. If wanting the shirt collar to be open as in a sports shirt, omit snap fasteners and buttons.

**TIMOTHY**   Two celluloid Baby Blue Eyes made in Japan in the 1930s, wearing the same suit made in different wools on different sized needles. The larger doll, which is 46 cm (18") long and was given to the author for her birthday in 1937, is the sleeping-eyed version of this popular celluloid doll. The smaller 32 cm (12½") doll with painted eyes is holding an English tin toy tractor by Mettoy. Pattern on page 54.

# *Timothy* *illustrated on page 52*

This boy doll's knitted suit in two sizes is ideally suited to celluloid dolls or bisque headed baby dolls.

## LARGER DOLL

### Materials
50 g (2 oz) Bendigo 3-ply fingering wool
Pair 3.75 mm (9) (US 5) needles
Length of elastic for pants
2 small buttons for jumper
Outfit can be knitted with other wool or materials, but may not register the same dimensions.

### Measurements:
| | |
|---|---|
| *Jumper* From top of shoulder | 16 cm (6¼") |
| Width around at underarm | 36 cm (14") |
| *Pants* Length at centre front | 16 cm (6¼") |
| *Beret* Circumference (unstretched) | 28 cm (10½") |
| *Shoes* Sole | 8.5 cm (3¼") |

### Tension
7 sts in width, 9 rows in depth = 2.5 cm (1") over smooth fabric.

## SMALLER DOLL

### Materials
25 g (1 oz) Bendigo 2-ply wool
Pair 2.75 mm (12) (US 2) needles
Length of elastic for pants
2 small buttons for jumper

### Measurements
| | |
|---|---|
| *Jumper* From top of shoulder | 13.5 cm (5¼") |
| Width around at underarm | 26 cm (10") + |
| *Pants* Length at centre front | 12.5 cm (4¾") |
| *Beret* Circumference (unstretched) | 20 cm (8") |
| *Shoes* Sole | 6 cm (2½") |

### Tension
9 sts in width, 12 rows in depth = 2.5 cm (1") of smooth fabric.

See page 10 for abbreviations.

The instructions for the smaller size are given in square brackets [].

## Jumper

*Front*

Using 3.75 mm (9) (US 5) [2.75 mm (12) (US 2)] needles throughout and wool to suit size required, cast on 48 sts and work 8 rows in k2, p2 rib, increasing 1 st at both ends of the last row of rib (50 sts).
Proceed in pattern as follows:
*1st row:* Sl 1 knitwise, k2, *p4, k4, rep from * to last three sts, k3.
*2nd row:* Sl 1 knitwise, purl to the last st, k1.
Repeat these 2 rows 14 times (30 rows from the beginning).
Shape armholes by casting off 3 sts at beginning of each of the next 2 rows.
K2 tog at both ends of every 2nd row until 40 sts remain, ending with a 2nd row.
Divide for front opening as follows:
Sl 1 knitwise, pattern 18, k2, turn.
Continue on these sts, keeping 2 sts in garter st at the front edge and making a buttonhole in the next and following 8th row as follows:
*Buttonhole row:* Sl 1 knitwise, k2 tog, wl rn, purl to the last st, k1.
After 2nd buttonhole has been worked, end at the front edge to shape neck.
Shape neck by casting off 8 sts at beginning of next row, then k2 tog at neck edge in next 2 rows (11 sts).
Work 7 rows in pattern. Cast off.
To work other side of front, cast on 2 sts at beginning of sts left on needle and work to correspond with left side, omitting buttonholes.

*Back*

Work exactly as for the front until the armhole shaping has been completed, then continue in pattern without shaping until the armholes correspond in length to the front armholes. Cast off.

*Sleeves*

Cast on 24 sts, and work 4 rows in k2, p2 rib, increasing 1 st at both ends of the last row of rib (26 sts).
Work in pattern as for front, increasing 1 st at both ends of the 3rd row and every following 4th row until there are 36 sts on the needle.
Work 5 rows straight in pattern. (If you want longer sleeves, work more rows at this point.)

To shape armholes and top:
K2 tog at both ends of every row until 20 sts remain. Cast off.
Work a second sleeve to match.

*Collar*
Cast on 50 sts, and work in k2, p2 rib, increasing 1 st at both ends of every 4th row, 4 times, then work 3 rows and cast off loosely in rib.

*To make up*
Join side, shoulder and sleeve seams. Sew in sleeves, placing seam to seam. Sew the cast-on sts for the under piece of front opening to back bottom of other side. Sew on collar, with cast-on stitches to neck, placing ends of collar to inside edge of front borders on each side. Press following instructions on page 6.

# Pants (knitted in one piece)

*Front*
Cast on 52 sts and work 4 rows in k2, p2 rib.
*5th row:* *Rib 2, wl fwd, k2 tog, repeat from * to end of row.
Work 3 more rows in rib, and then work 26 rows in stocking st.
Shape gusset as follows:
*1st row:* Sl 1 knitwise, k24, (k1, p1) into each of next 2 sts, knit to end of row (54 sts).
*2nd and alternate rows:* Sl 1 knitwise, purl to last st, k1.
*3rd row:* Sl 1 knitwise, knit to end.
*5th row:* Sl 1 knitwise, k24, (k1, p1) into next st, k2, (k1, p1) into next st, knit to end.
Repeat 2nd, 3rd and 4th rows once.
*9th row:* Sl 1 knitwise, k24, (k1, p1) into the next st, k4, (k1, p1) into next st, knit to end.
Repeat 2nd, 3rd, and 4th rows.
*13th row:* Sl 1 knitwise, k24, (k1, p1) into next st, k6, (k1, p1) into next st, knit to end (60 sts).
Repeat 2nd, 3rd, and 4th rows.
*17th row:* Sl 1 knitwise, k24, (k1, p1) into next st, k8, (k1, p1) into next st, knit to end (62 sts).
Purl 1 row.
Cast off 26 sts at the beginning of each of the next 2 rows for the leg openings, then cast on 26 sts at the end of the next two rows (62 sts).
Decrease for the second half of the gusset as follows:
*1st row:* Sl 1 knitwise, k24, k2 tog, k8, k2 tog, knit to end.
*2nd row:* Sl 1 knitwise, purl to last st, k1.
*3rd row:* Sl 1 knitwise, knit to end.
*4th row:* As 2nd row.
*5th row:* Sl 1 knitwise, k24, k2 tog, k6, k2 tog, knit to end (58 sts).

Repeat 2nd, 3rd and 4th rows.
*9th row:* Sl 1 knitwise, k24, k2 tog, k4, k2 tog, knit to end (56 sts).
Repeat 2nd, 3rd, and 4th rows.
*13th row:* Sl 1 knitwise, k24, k2 tog, k2, k2 tog, knit to end (54 sts).
Repeat 2nd, 3rd and 4th rows.
*17th row:* Sl 1 knitwise, k24, k2 tog, k2 tog, knit to end (52 sts).
Continue in stocking st without further shaping until back is the same length as front to ribbing (25 rows), ending with a purl row.
Shape back as follows:
Sl 1 knitwise, k43, turn.
Purl 36 sts, turn.
Knit 28 sts, turn.
Purl 20 sts, turn and knit to end of row.
Work 3 rows in k2, p2 rib.
Make holes for elastic as follows:
Rib 2, wl fwd, ml, k2 tog, repeat from * to end of row.
Work 4 rows in rib and cast off in rib.
With right side of work facing, knit up 52 sts along one leg opening. Work 6 rows in k2, p2 rib. Cast off loosely in rib.
Work other leg opening in the same way.

*To make up*
Press following instructions on page 6.
Join side seams and thread elastic through the holes in waist.

# Beret

Cast on 70 sts, and work 6 rows in k1, p1 rib, increasing 1 st on the last row (71 sts).
Continue as follows:
*1st row:* Sl 1 knitwise, * inc in next st, k9, repeat from * to end.
*2nd and alternate rows:* Sl 1 knitwise, purl to last st, k1.
*3rd row:* Sl 1 knitwise, * inc in next st, k10, repeat from * to end.
*5th row:* Sl 1 knitwise, * inc in next st, k11, repeat from * to end.
Continue in this way, increasing 7 sts on every knit row, until there are 106 sts, ending with a purl row.
Work 4 rows in garter st then decrease for the crown as follows:
*1st row:* Sl 1 knitwise, * k13, k2 tog, repeat from * to end.
*2nd row:* * p2 tog, p12, repeat from * to end, k1.
*3rd row:* Sl 1 knitwise, * k11, k2 tog, repeat from * to end.
*4th and all alternate rows:* Sl 1 knitwise, purl to last st, k1.
*5th row:* Sl 1 knitwise, * k10, k2 tog, repeat from * to end.
*7th row:* Sl 1 knitwise, * k9, k2 tog, repeat from * to end.

Continue to decrease, working 1 st less between the decreases until 22 sts remain.

*Next row:* Sl 1 knitwise, k1, k2 tog, repeat from * to end of row.

Break off wool, thread onto darning needle, thread wool through remaining sts and draw up and fasten off. Join up seam and press.

# Shoes

The instructions given for the shoes with the original pattern are for a doll with rather large feet. If the shoes are too large for your doll, try making them on needles one or even two sizes smaller, as they are quite a nice shoe.

Cast on 20 sts, and work in garter st, increasing at the beginning of every 2nd row until there are 26 sts, ending at the straight edge.

Cast off 12 sts at the beginning of the next row for the side, then work 7 rows without shaping, ending at the edge where the sts were cast off.

Cast on 12 sts at this edge for the other side, knitting 2 sts tog at the opposite edge on every 2nd row until 20 sts remain, ending at the straight edge.

*Next row:* Cast off 4 sts, knit to end.

Now work on the remaining sts for the sole, increasing 1 st at both ends of the next and following 2nd row (20 sts). Work 4 rows without shaping, then k2 tog at both ends of the next and following 2nd row (16 sts). Cast off.

*Button strap*

Join the straight edges of the sides to form the back seam. Cast 12 sts onto your needle, then with the outside of the slipper facing, knit up 10 sts (5 sts on each side of the back seam), cast on 12 sts (34 sts).

Knit 1 row.

*Next row:* Sl 1 knitwise, k1, wl fwd, k2 tog, knit to the end. Cast off.

Work a second shoe in the same way, making the buttonhole at the opposite end of the strap.

*To make up*

Placing the centre of the edge of the sole to the back seam, sew round the back, the sides and toe, easing in the top to fit without stretching the edge of the sole. Sew a button to each strap to match the buttonhole.

# *Trevor* *illustrated on page 39*

A delightful three-piece outfit of cap, shirt and short pants to suit a small doll of 18–19 cm (7"–7½"). Needing only a small amount of material, the whole outfit can be made in a matter of a few hours.

## Materials:
Small ball 3-ply baby wool in white or a light colour for the shirt
25 g (1 oz) baby wool in a darker colour for the pants and cap
Pair 2 mm (14) (US 0) knitting needles
3 tiny buttons for the shirt
Length of hat elastic for the pants

## Measurements:

| | |
|---|---|
| *Shirt:* From top of shoulder | 6 cm (2¼") |
| Width around at underarm (fastened) | 14 cm (5½") |
| Length of sleeve to underarm | 2.5 cm (1") |
| *Pants:* Length of front seam | 5 cm (2") |
| Length of inside leg | 1.5 cm (½") |
| *Cap:* Circumference (unstretched) | 13 cm (5") |

## Tension
8 sts in width to 2 cm (¾"), 11 rows in depth to 2 cm (¾").

See page 10 for abbreviations.

## Pants

*Back*
Using 2 mm (14) (US 0) needles and 3-ply baby wool in darker shade, cast on 26 sts and work 4 rows in k1, p1 rib. Working in stocking st, inc 1 st at each end of the next row, and every following 4th row, three times (32 sts). (If you want a shorter pair of pants, work less rows between incs.)
Purl 1 row.
To shape the legs:
Dec 1 st at each end of the next 4 rows (24 sts).
To work the gusset:
*1st row:* k2 tog, k9, (inc in the next st) twice, k9, k2 tog.
*2nd and following 3 alternate rows:* p2 tog, purl until 2 sts remain, p2 tog.
*3rd row:* k2 tog, k7, inc, k2, inc, k7, k2 tog.
*5th row:* k2 tog, k5, inc, k4, inc, k5, k2 tog.
*7th row:* k2 tog, k3, inc, k6, inc, k3, k2 tog.
*9th row:* k2 tog, k1, inc, k8, inc, k1, k2 tog.
*10th row:* Cast off using purl.
Make another piece the same, and join under the crutch.
Thread a length of hat elastic through ribbing at waist.

## Shirt

*Back*
Using white or light coloured wool cast on 26 sts, and work 6 rows in k1, p1 rib.
*Next row:* Inc 3 sts along row, (1 inc at each end and 1 inc in the middle) (29 sts).
*1st row:* Knit (wrong side).
*2nd row:* k1, p1.
These last 2 rows form the pattern. Repeat the pattern rows, 4 times.
To shape the armholes:
Cast off 4 sts at the beginning of the next 2 rows (21 sts).
Work 10 rows in pattern (5 patterns).
To shape shoulders:
Cast off 7 sts at the beginning of next 2 rows.
Cast off remaining 7 sts.

*Right front*
Cast on 16 sts with white wool.
*1st row:* k4, *k1, p1, repeat from * to end of row.
*2nd row:* k1, p1, to last 4 sts, k4.
*3rd row* (buttonhole): k2, m1, k2 tog, *k1, p1, repeat from * to end of row.
*4th row:* As 2nd row.
Repeat 1st and 2nd row once.
*7th row:* k4, inc, work 6 sts in rib, inc, work in rib to end.
*8th row* (wrong side): Knit.
*9th row:* k4, * p1, k1, repeat from * to end of row.
Repeat 8th and 9th rows twice.
*2nd buttonhole row:* k4, m1, k2 tog, * p1, k1, repeat from * to end.
Repeat 8th and 9th rows twice.
To shape armhole:
Cast off 4 sts at the beginning of the next row, then continue in pattern for 4 rows.
*Buttonhole row:* k4, m1, k2 tog, * p1, k1, repeat from * to end.
*Next row:* Knit.
To shape neck:
Working in pattern as set, cast off 4 sts at the beginning of the next row, then dec 1 st at the neck edge of the next 3 rows.
Work 2 rows in pattern. Cast off.

*Left front*
Cast on 16 sts.
*1st row:* k1, p1, to last 4 sts, k4.
*2nd row:* k4, * k1, p1, repeat from * to end.
Repeat 1st and 2nd rows twice.
*Inc row:* Inc in 1st st, work in rib to last 5 sts, inc, k4.
Work 10 rows in pattern as given for back, keeping the 4 st garter st border at front edge.
To shape armholes:
Cast off 4 sts at the beginning of the next row (14 sts).
Continue in pattern for the next 6 rows.
Shape neck as for the right front.

*Sleeves*
With white wool cast on 18 sts, and work 4 rows in k1, p1 rib.
Work 4 rows in pattern, and then inc at each end of the next row (20 sts).
Keeping pattern correct, work 3 rows.
To shape the sleeve:
Cast off 3 sts at beginning of next 2 rows (14 sts), and then dec 1 st at the beginning of the next 6 rows (8 sts). Cast off.
Make another sleeve the same.

*Collar*
Cast on 37 sts, and work 2 rows in garter st.
Dec 1 st at each end of the next 2 rows.
Work 1 row in garter st. Cast off.

*To make up*
As the pattern can be used with either side out, decide which side you like before starting to make up the garment. Press following instructions on page 6. Sew up shoulder seams, set sleeves into armholes, then join sleeve and side seams as one. Sew the cast-off edge of the collar to the neck edge, and finish by sewing 3 small buttons to correspond with the buttonholes.
If you want short sleeves, turn back the ribbed cuff of each sleeve.

# Cap

Cast on 50 sts and work 8 rows in k1, p1 rib.
Work 8 rows in stocking st.
*9th row:* Dec 1 st each end of next row.
*10th row:* Purl.
*11th row:* * k6, k2 tog, repeat from * to end of row.
*12th and all alternate rows:* Purl.
*13th row:* *k5, k2 tog, repeat from * to end of row.
*15th row:* * k4, k2 tog, repeat from * to end of row.
Continue as set, working less sts between the k2 togs, until you have finished the row k1, k2 tog. Break off wool, leaving an end to thread through remaining 12 sts. Fasten off tightly and sew up seam.

# Bibliography

Allen, Ella: *Dress Your Dolly in Knitting and Crochet*, (1932) published by The Speciality Press Pty Ltd, Melbourne

*Dolly's Outfit* Booklet (*c.* 1900–1910) from Scotch Wool and Hosiery Stores

*Dolls' Woolly Outfits* (1939–40) Bairnswear Booklet No. 181

*Knitted Set for a Boy Doll* (1914) Girls Own Annual, London

*Knitted Sets for Dolls* (*c.* 1930s) booklet published by Fitchett Bros. Pty Ltd, Melbourne

'Outdoor Set for a Baby Doll' *English Woman's Weekly* December 9, 1939

Patons Knitting Book No. C 5 (1953, reprinted 1955)

Patons Knitting Book No. C 13 (1959)

Patons Knitting Book No 252

Speciality Gift and Craft Book No. 43, Patons & Baldwins

# Suppliers

Look in your local phone book under the Craft section if no other classification seems appropriate.

Coats Patons wool is available in most shops specialising in wool, and also in the haberdashery departments of large stores such as Myers, David Jones, Big W and K-Mart.

You may find also wools from England in the 2-ply, 3-ply and 4-ply range in many of the specialised wool shops in the southern states of Australia and overseas. Finer wools such as 1-ply can be obtained from miniature (dollhouse) outlets.

Bendigo Woollen Mills offer a speedy mail order service to their customers, and take most major credit cards. They will willingly send you a sample card of their wools and the colours available for each ply.

*Australia*
Bendigo Woollen Mills
Lansell Street,
Bendigo, Victoria 3550
Phone (054) 42 4600*
* number may change after July 1995

*United States*
Bendigo Woollen Mills
PO Box 27164
Columbus, Ohio 43227
Phone 614 236 9112

Miniature Design Co.
PO Box 438
Woodridge, Queensland 4114
Phone (07) 209 5672

For fine knitting needles sizes 14–20 and 1-ply wool in all shades, also 1-ply nylon, crepe and mohair. Mail order.

# Index